Additional Practice and Skills Workbook

Grade 7

Glenda Lappan
James T. Fey
William M. Fitzgerald
Susan Friel
Elizabeth Difanis Phillips

PEARSON

Prentice
Hall

Boston, Massachusetts
Upper Saddle River, New Jersey

Connected Mathematics™ Project was developed at Michigan State University with financial support from the Michigan State University Office of the Provost, Computing and Technology, and the College of Natural Science.

Connected Mathematics™ is based upon work supported by the National Science Foundation under Grant No. MDR 9150217 and Grant No. ESI 9986372. Opinions expressed are those of the authors and not necessarily those of the Foundation.

The Michigan State University authors and administration have agreed that all MSU royalties arising from this publication will be devoted to purposes supported by the Department of Mathematics and the MSU Mathematics Enrichment Fund.

Acknowledgments The people who made up the *Connected Mathematics 2* team—representing editorial, editorial services, design services, and production services—are listed below. Bold type denotes core team members.

Leora Adler, Judith Buice, Kerry Cashman, Patrick Culleton, Sheila DeFazio, Katie Hallahan, Richard Heater, **Barbara Holllingdale, Jayne Holman,** Karen Holtzman, **Etta Jacobs,** Christine Lee, Carolyn Lock, Catherine Maglio, **Dotti Marshall,** Rich McMahon, Eve Melnechuk, Terri Mitchell, **Marsha Novak,** Irene Rubin, Donna Russo, Robin Samper, Siri Schwartzman, **Nancy Smith,** Emily Soltanoff, **Mark Tricca,** Paula Vergith, Roberta Warshaw, Helen Young.

ISBN 0-13-165615-5

8 9 10   09 08 07

Table of Contents

Accentuate the Negative

Moving Straight Ahead

Filling and Wrapping

Additional Practice

1. a. The graph below shows the relationship between two variables. What are the variables?

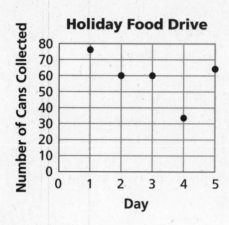

Holiday Food Drive

b. On which day were the most cans of food collected? How many cans were collected on that day?

c. What total number of cans was collected over the 5 days? Explain your reasoning.

d. What is the mean number of cans collected over the five days? Explain your reasoning.

e. On this graph, does it make sense to connect the points with line segments? Explain your reasoning.

Additional Practice (continued)

2. Emma and her mother go walking one evening. Emma keeps track of their pace over their hour and ten-minute walk. She made the following notes:

- We started at 7:00 PM and walked quickly for 15 minutes.
- We stopped for 5 minutes to talk to a friend.
- We walked slowly for 20 minutes to look at the neighbor's yards.
- At 7:40, we stopped for 15 minutes to get an ice cream cone.
- We walked back at a slow pace for 10 minutes.
- Then we walked very quickly for 5 minutes (speed walking).
- We got back at 8:10 and had walked 2 miles.

a. Make a table of (time, distance) data that reasonably fits the information in Emma's notes.

b. Sketch a coordinate graph that shows the same information as the table.

c. Does it make sense to connect the points on this graph? Explain your reasoning.

d. If Emma decided to only show one method of displaying the data (time, distance) to her mother, which should she choose if she wanted to show her mother the changes in their walking speed? Explain your choice.

Additional Practice (continued)

3. a. Andrew's mother kept the chart below of the number of words his sister Sarah could say at the end of each month from age 1 month to 24 months. Sarah did not say a word until 12 months, so from 1 to 11 Andrew's mother wrote 0. Make a coordinate graph of these data. Explain how you chose the variables for each axis.

Age (months)	Number of Words Sarah can Say
1–11	0
12	1
13	1
14	2
15	3
16	7
17	10
18	15
19	24
20	28
21	30
22	47
23	51
24	62

b. Describe how the number of words Sarah can say changed as she got older (as the number of months passed).

c. During what month did Sarah learn to say the most words? The least (not counting from 1 to 11 months?

Additional Practice *(continued)*

4. The Student Council of Metropolis Middle School voted on seven different proposals related to school activities. There are nine students on the Student Council and each student voted "yes" or "no" for each proposal. Use the information in the table at the right to answer parts (a)–(d).

   School Activity Proposals

Proposal	Yes Votes
1	6
2	9
3	3
4	8
5	6
6	5
7	7

   a. What are the variables shown in the table?

   b. Which variable is the independent variable and which is the dependent variable? Explain your reasoning.

   c. Make a coordinate graph of the data in the table. Label your *x*-axis and *y*-axis with the correct independent or dependent variable.

   d. Make a coordinate graph showing how many students voted "no" on each of the seven proposals. Explain how you find the data for your graph. Label the *x*-axis and *y*-axis with the appropriate independent or dependent variable.

Additional Practice (continued)

5. Below is a chart of the water depth in a harbor during a typical 24-hour day. The water level rises and falls with the tide.

Hours Since Midnight	0	1	2	3	4	5	6	7	8	9	10	11	12
Depth (meters)	8.4	8.9	9.9	10.7	11.2	12.1	12.9	12.2	11.3	10.6	9.4	8.3	8.0

Hours Since Midnight	13	14	15	16	17	18	19	20	21	22	23	24
Depth (meters)	8.4	9.4	10.8	11.4	12.2	13.0	12.4	11.3	10.4	9.8	8.6	8.1

a. Make a coordinate graph of the data.

b. During which time interval(s) does the depth of the water increase the most?

c. During which time interval(s) does the depth of the water decrease the most?

d. Would it make sense to connect the points on the graph? Why or why not?

e. Is it easier to use the table or the graph to answer parts (b) and (c)? Explain.

Additional Practice (continued)

6. Make a table and a graph of (time, temperature) data that fit the following information about a day on the road:

   • We started riding at 9:00 A.M. once the fog had burned off. The day was quite cool. The temperature was 52°F, and the sun was shining brightly.

   • About midmorning, the temperature rose to 70°F and cloud cover moved in, which kept the temperature steady until lunch time.

   • Suddenly the sun burst through the clouds, and the temperature began to climb. By late afternoon, it was 80°F.

7. Make a graph that shows your hunger level over the course of a day. Label the *x*-axis from 6 A.M. to midnight. Write a story about what happened during the day in relation to your hunger level.

Skill: Tables and Graphs

1. a. Graph the data in the table.

100-megabyte Computer Disks

Number of disks	Price (dollars)
1	20
2	37
3	50
6	100
10	150

b. Use the graph to estimate the cost of five disks.

2. a. The table shows average monthly temperatures in degrees Fahrenheit for American cities in January and July. Graph the data in the table.

City	Seattle	Baltimore	Boise	Chicago	Dallas	Miami	LA
Jan.	39.1	32.7	29.9	21.4	44.0	67.1	56.0
Jul.	64.8	76.8	74.6	73.0	86.3	82.5	69.0

City	Anchorage	Honolulu	New York	Portland	New Orleans
Jan.	13.0	72.6	31.8	21.5	52.4
Jul.	58.1	80.1	76.4	68.1	82.1

b. Use your graph to estimate the July temperature of a city whose average January temperature is 10°F.

Additional Practice

1. When the *Ocean Bike Tour* operators considered leasing a small bus for the summer season, they checked prices from two companies.

   a. East Coast Transport (ECT) would charge $1,000 plus $2.50 per mile that their bus would be driven. Make a table showing the cost of leasing from ECT for 100, 200, 300, 400, 500, 600, 700, 800, 900, and 1,000 miles of driving.

   b. Superior Buses would charge only $5 per mile that their bus would be driven. Make a table showing the cost of leasing from Superior Buses for 100, 200, 300, 400, 500, 600, 700, 800, 900, and 1,000 miles of driving.

   c. On one coordinate grid, plot the charge plans for both bus-leasing companies. Use different colors to mark each company's plan.

   d. Why, if at all, does it make sense to connect the dots on your plots of part (c)?

   e. Based on your work in parts (a)–(c), which lease option seems best? How is your answer supported by data in the tables and patterns in the graphs?

Additional Practice *(continued)*

2. a. A newspaper included the graph below in a story about the amount of city land used for trash between 2000 and 2005. The graph shows the relationship between two variables. What are they?

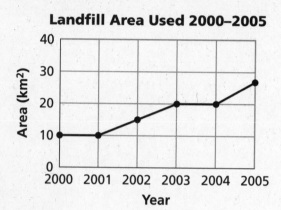

Landfill Area Used 2000–2005

b. What is the difference between the least and greatest amount of land used for trash?

c. Between which two years did the area used for trash stay the same?

d. On this graph, what information is given by the lines connecting the points? Is this information necessarily accurate? Explain your reasoning.

e. In 2000, the total area available for trash was 120 square kilometers. Make a coordinate graph that shows the landfill area remaining in each year from 2000 to 2005.

Additional Practice *(continued)*

3. a. Make a coordinate graph of these data.

Roller Rink Fees

Minutes	Cost
30	$3.50
60	$7.00
90	$10.50
120	$14.00
150	$17.50
180	$21.00

b. Would it make sense to connect the points on your graph? Why or why not?

c. Using the table, describe the pattern of change in the total skating fee as the number of minutes increases. How is this pattern shown in the graph?

4. a. A roller-blade supply store rents roller blades for $2.50 per skater. Using increments of 5 skaters, make a table showing the total rental charge for 0 to 50 skaters. Make a coordinate graph of these data.

b. Compare the pattern of change in your table and graph with the patterns you found in the skating fees in Exercise 3. Describe any similarities and differences.

Additional Practice (continued)

5. a. Use the graph to make a table of data showing the sales for each month.

b. The profit made by the concession stand is half of the sales. Make a table of data that shows the profit made by the concession stand for each month.

Additional Practice (continued)

c. Make a coordinate graph of the data from part (b). Use the same scale used in the sales graph above. Describe how the sales graph and the profit graph are similar and how they are different.

6. The three graphs below show the progress of a cyclist at different times during a ride. For each graph, describe the rider's progress over the time interval.

a.

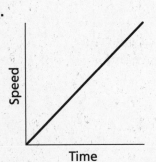

b.

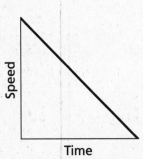

c.

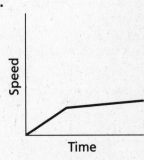

Skill: Analyzing Graphs

Graphs I through VI represent one of the six situations described below. Match each graph with the situation that describes it.

I.

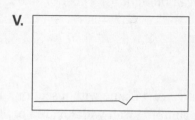

II.

III.

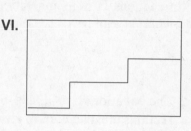

IV.

V.

VI.

1. temperature as the weather changes from rainy to snowy

2. number of fish caught per hour on a bad fishing day

3. total rainfall during a rainy day

4. speed of a car starting from a stop sign and then approaching a stoplight

5. height of a cricket as it jumps

6. total amount of money spent over time during a trip to the mall

Sketch a graph for each situation.

7. The speed of a runner in a 1-mi race.

8. The height above ground of the air valve on a tire of a bicycle ridden on flat ground. (You can model this using a coin.)

Additional Practice

1. Use equations relating to building and cost plans for the Wild World climbing wall to answer parts (a)–(d).

   a. The equation $B = 1 + 3n$ tells the number of beams required to build a frame of n sections. How many sections can be built with 79 beams?

   b. The equation $C = 100 + 300n$ tells the cost of building a frame of n sections. How many sections can be built for a cost of \$4,000? How high will that wall be?

   c. The equation $A = 4n$ tells the area of a frame with n sections. How many sections must be built to give a climbing wall with an area of 96 square meters?

   d. The equation $L = 4n + 2$ gives the length of the light string needed for side and top edges of a climbing wall with n sections in its frame. What size frame (number of sections) can be lighted with a string that is 38 meters long?

2. In parts (a)–(e), use symbols to express the rule as the equation. Use single letters to stand for the variables. Identify what each letter represents.

   a. The perimeter of a rectangle is twice its length plus twice its width.

   b. The area of a triangle is one-half its base multiplied by its height.

   c. Three big marshmallows are needed to make each s'more.

   d. The number of quarters in an amount of money expressed in dollars is four times the number of dollars.

   e. A half-cup of unpopped popcorn is needed to make 6 cups of popped popcorn.

Additional Practice (continued)

3. The equation $d = 44t$ represents the distance in miles covered, after traveling 44 miles per hour for t hours.

  a. Make a table that shows the distance traveled, according to this equation, for every half hour between 0 and 4 hours.

  b. Sketch a graph that shows the distance traveled between 0 and 4 hours.

  c. If $t = 2.5$, what is d?

  d. If $d = 66$, what is t?

  e. Does it make sense to connect the points on this graph with line segments? Why or why not?

Additional Practice (continued)

4. a. The number of students at Smithville Middle School is 21 multiplied by the number of teachers. Use symbols to express the rule relating the number of students and the number of teachers as an equation. Use single letters for your variables and explain what each letter represents.

b. If there are 50 teachers at Smithville Middle School, how many students attend the school?

c. If 1,260 students attend Smithville Middle School, how many teachers teach at the school?

5. a. Refer to the table below. Use symbols to express the rule relating the side length of a square to its area as an equation. Use single letters for your variables, and explain what each letter represents.

Squares

Side Length (cm)	Area (cm²)
1	1
1.5	2.25
2	4
2.5	6.25
3	9
■	■
■	■
■	■

b. Use your equation to find the area of a square with a side length of 6 centimeters.

c. Use your equation to find the side length of a square with an area of 1.44 square centimeters.

Skill: Variables, Tables, and Graphs

Complete each table given the rule.

Rule: Output = Input · 5

1.

Input	1	2	3	4	5
Output	5	10	15		

Rule: Output = Input · 2

2.

Input	10	20	30	40	50
Output	20	40	60		

Rule: Output = Input + 3

3.

Input	3	4	5	6	7
Output	6	7	8		

Graph the data in each table.

4.

Hours	Wages
1	$15
2	$30
3	$45
4	$60

5.

Gallons	Quarts
1	4
2	8
3	12
4	16

6. A parking garage charges $3.50 per hour to park. The equation $c = 3.5h$ shows how the number of hours h relates to the parking charge c. Graph this relationship.

Use the expression to complete each table.

7.

x	$x + 7$
2	9
5	12
8	
11	
	21

8.

x	$5x$
3	
6	
9	
12	
	75

9.

x	$125 - x$
15	
30	
45	
60	
	50

Skill: Variables, Tables, and Graphs *(continued)*

10. A cellular phone company charges a $49.99 monthly fee for 600 free
minutes. Each additional minute costs $0.35. This month you used
750 minutes. How much do you owe?

Write a rule for the relationship between the variables represented in each table.

11.

x	y
1	6
2	7
3	8
4	9

12.

x	y
1	4
2	8
3	12
4	16

13.

x	y
1	4
2	7
3	10
4	13

14. A typist types 45 words per minute.

 a. Write a rule to represent the relationship between the number of typed
 words and the time in which they are typed.

 b. How many words can the typist type in 25 minutes? Write and solve an
 equation to answer this.

 c. How long would it take the typist to type 20,025 words?

Additional Practice

1. For each set of (x, y) coordinates, find a pattern in the data and express the rule for the pattern as an equation.

   a. $(0, 0), (1, 0.5), (2, 1), (3, 1.5), (6, 3), (10, 5), (21, 10.5), (1000, 500)$

   b. $(1, 2), (2, 5), (3, 8), (4, 11), (5, 14), (10, 29), (100, 299)$

   c. $(0, 4), (1, 5), (2, 8), (3, 13), (4, 20), (5, 29), (6, 40), (7, 53), (10, 104)$

2. Enter each of the equations from Exercise 1 into your graphing calculator. Describe the graph of each equation. How do the three graphs compare?

3. Graph the equations $y = 2x - 1$ and $y = x$ in the same window of your graphing calculator. Make a sketch of the window.

   a. Do the graphs of the two equations intersect? If they do, give the (x, y) coordinates of the point(s) where the graphs intersect.

   b. Do you think it is possible for two different lines to intersect at more than one point?

   c. Use your graphing calculator to find two equations whose graphs do not intersect.

Additional Practice (continued)

4. a. A Student Council wants to throw a party for students. They decide to have a breakfast catered and they compare bids of two companies. The Catering Crew charges $8 per student. Urbandale Catering Company charges a set fee of $160 plus $6 per student. Make tables that show costs for each company in cases where 20, 40, 60, 80, 100, and 120 students would attend.

   b. Plot the (*number of students*, *catering costs*) on a graph. Use different colors or plotting symbols for points to show the two catering companies.

   c. Write equations relating total cost and number of students for each catering company.

   d. Use your graphing calculator to graph each of the equations on the same axes. Compare these graphs to those you did by hand.

   e. Is there any number of students for which both companies would charge the same rental fee?

   f. If 60 students signed up to come to the breakfast, which company should the Student Council select? What if 100 students signed up for the breakfast?

Additional Practice

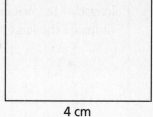

Stretching and Shrinking

1. Refer to the rectangle at the right to answer the following questions.

   a. Give the length and width of a larger similar rectangle. Explain your reasoning.

   b. Give the length and width of a smaller similar rectangle. Explain your reasoning.

   c. Give the length and width of a rectangle that is *not* similar to this one. Explain your reasoning.

3 cm

4 cm

2. Figure *VWXYZ* is an enlargement of figure *ABCDE*. Name all the pairs of corresponding sides and all the pairs of corresponding angles of the two figures.

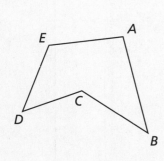
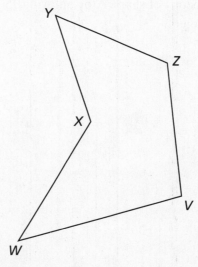

21

Additional Practice (continued)

3. a. Draw a square. Then draw a square with a side length that is twice the side length of the original square. How many copies of the smaller square will fit inside the larger square?

b. Will you get the same answer for part (a) no matter what side length you choose for the original square? Explain your reasoning.

4. a. Carl made shape B by making a photocopy of shape A. What percent did he enter in the copier?

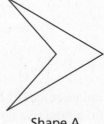

Shape A   Shape B

b. Amy made a photocopy of shape A by entering 250% into the photocopier. Sketch the copy she got.

Skill: Using Percent

Find the given percent of each number. Show your work.

1. 20% of 560

2. 42% of 200

3. 9% of 50

4. 40% of 70

5. 25% of 80

6. 50% of 80

7. 40% of 200

8. 5% of 80

9. 75% of 200

Additional Practice

1. Draw any rectangle that is not a square. Draw a similar rectangle by applying a scale factor of 3 to the original rectangle.

   a. How many copies of the original rectangle will fit inside the new rectangle?

   b. Will you get the same answer for part (a) no matter what rectangle you use as the original rectangle?

2. Make a figure by connecting the following sets of points on a coordinate grid:

   Set 1: (8,5), (8,8), (0,8), (0,5), (8,5)   Set 2: (4,6), (8,2), (0,2), (4,6)

   Set 3: (2,6), (1,6), (1, 7), (2,7), (2,6)   Set 4: (6,6), (7,6), (7,7), (6,7), (6,6)

   a. Suppose you used the rule $(6x, 6y)$ to transform this figure into a new figure. How would the angles of the new figure compare with the angles of the original?

   b. Suppose you used the rule $(6x, 6y)$ to transform this figure into a new figure. How would the side lengths of the new figure compare to the side lengths of the original?

Additional Practice (continued)

c. Suppose you used the rule $(6x, 6y)$ to transform this figure into a new figure. Would the new figure be similar to the original? Explain your reasoning.

d. Suppose you used the rule $(3x+1, 3y-4)$ to transform the original figure into a new figure. How would the angles of the new figure compare with the angles of the original?

e. Suppose you used the rule $(3x+1, 3y-4)$ to transform the original figure into a new figure. How would the side lengths of the new figure compare to the side lengths of the original?

f. Suppose you used the rule $(3x+1, 3y-4)$ to transform the original figure into a new figure. Would the new figure be similar to the original? Explain.

3. Recall that Zug Wump was made from Mug Wump using a scale factor of 2. What is the scale factor from Zug to Mug? Explain.

4. a. Wendy drew a very large Wump using the rule $(8x, 8y)$. She said that the scale factor from Mug to her Wump was 8 and that the scale factor from Zug to her Wump was 4. Do you agree with Wendy? Explain.

b. Wendy could not figure out the scale factor from Bug Wump to her new large Wump. What is this scale factor?

Name _____ Date _____ Class _____

Skill: Similar Figures

Tell whether the triangles are *similar*.

1.   2.  3.

4. List the pairs of figures that appear to be similar.

a.   b.   c.   d.

e.   f.   g. 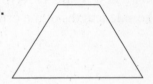 h.

For Exercises 5 and 6, graph the coordinates of the quadrilateral *ABCD*. Find the coordinates of its image *A′B′C′D′* with the given scale factor.

5. $A(2, -2), B(3, 2), C(-3, 2), D(-2, -2)$; scale factor 2

6. $A(6, 3), B(0, 6), C(-6, 2), D(-6, -5)$; scale factor $\frac{1}{2}$

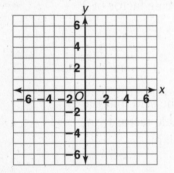 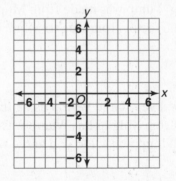

7. Quadrilateral $A′B′C′D′$ is similar to quadrilateral $ABCD$. Find the scale factor.

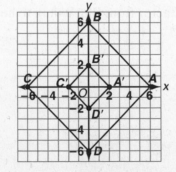

26

Additional Practice

1. a. On grid paper, make a right triangle with legs of length 8 and 12.

   b. Give the leg lengths of two smaller right triangles that are similar to the one you drew and that have whole-number side lengths.

   c. Copies of each smaller triangle can be put together to exactly match the original triangle. How many of each smaller triangle does it take to match the original?

2. On centimeter-grid paper, make an isosceles triangle with base and height both equal to 6 centimeters.

   a. Can isosceles triangles with base and height equal to 2 centimeters be put together to exactly match the shape of the original triangle? Is each smaller triangle similar to the original?

   b. Can isosceles triangles with base and height equal to 4 centimeters be put together to exactly match the shape of the original triangle? Is each smaller triangle similar to the original?

   c. Can copies of the triangle below be put together to exactly match the shape of your original isosceles triangle? Is this triangle similar to the original?

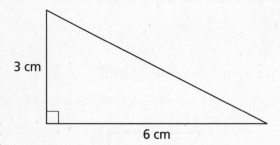

3 cm
6 cm

3. Find the missing values in each pair of similar figures below.

   a.

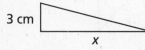

3 cm x 2 cm   8 cm

   b.

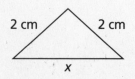

2 cm   2 cm
x

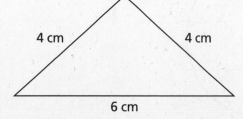

4 cm   4 cm
6 cm

Additional Practice (continued)

4. a. The drawing below shows how a square foot and a square yard compare. How many square feet are in a square yard? Explain your reasoning.

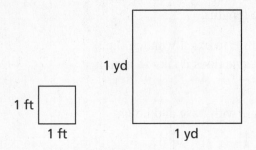

1 yd

1 ft

1 ft   1 yd

b. Are a square foot and a square yard similar? If so, what is the scale factor from a square foot to a square yard? What is the scale factor from a square yard to a square foot?

c. Compare a square inch with a square foot. What is the scale factor from a square inch to a square foot?

d. How many square inches are in a square foot? Explain.

e. Compare a square inch with a square yard. What is the scale factor from a square inch to a square yard?

f. How many square inches are in a square yard?

5. For each pair of figures below, give the scale factor from figure A to figure B.

a.

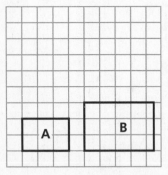

b.

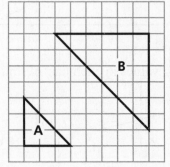

c.

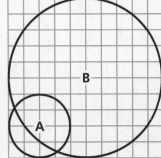

Skill: Similar Polygons

Stretching and Shrinking

The pairs of figures below are similar. Find the value of each variable.

1.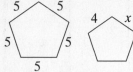

2.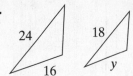

3.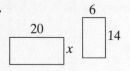

4.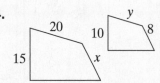

5.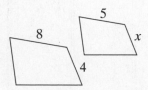

6.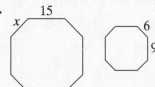

Skill: Fractions, Decimals, and Percents

Write three equivalent fractions for each fraction.

1. $\frac{3}{10}$

2. $\frac{7}{8}$

3. $\frac{5}{6}$

4. $\frac{3}{4}$

5. $\frac{15}{20}$

6. $\frac{8}{12}$

7. $\frac{15}{45}$

8. $\frac{8}{32}$

Write each fraction as a decimal and as a percent.

9. $\frac{3}{5}$

10. $\frac{7}{10}$

11. $\frac{13}{25}$

12. $\frac{17}{20}$

Additional Practice

1. a. Rachel was working with the triangles below:

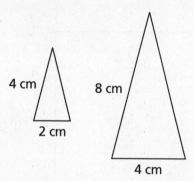

She wrote the fraction $\frac{1}{2}$. What was she thinking about?

b. Next, she wrote the fraction $\frac{1}{3}$ while working with these two triangles:

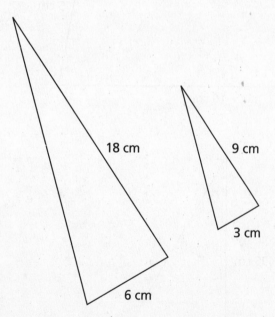

Was she thinking in the same way or differently? Explain.

Additional Practice *(continued)*

2. Below are several pairs of similar figures. In each, find the missing measurement(s).

a.

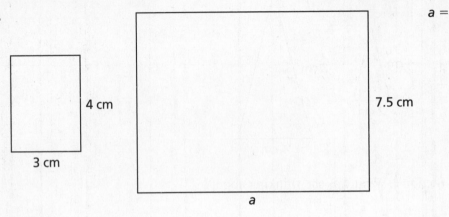

a =

4 cm

7.5 cm

3 cm

a

b.

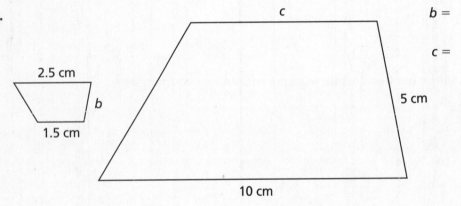

b =

c =

c

2.5 cm

b

5 cm

1.5 cm

10 cm

c.

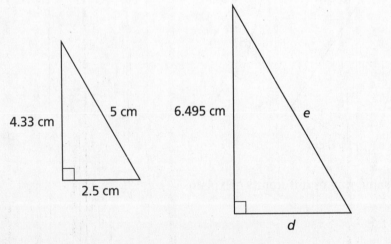

d =

e =

4.33 cm

5 cm

6.495 cm

e

2.5 cm

d

Additional Practice (continued)

3. In each figure below, find the missing measurement.

a.

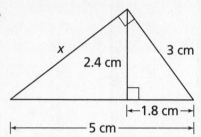

$x =$

b.

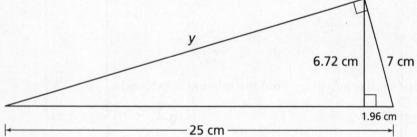

$y =$

Skill: Similarity and Ratios

Tell whether each pair of polygons is similar. Explain why or why not.

1.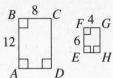

2.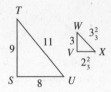

3.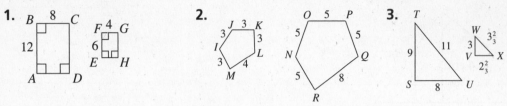

4.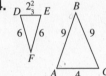

5.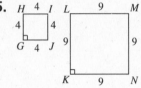

6.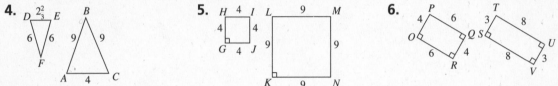

Exercise 7–11 show pairs of similar polygons. Find the missing side lengths.

7.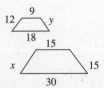

8.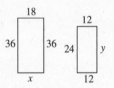

9.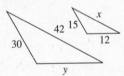

10.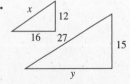

11.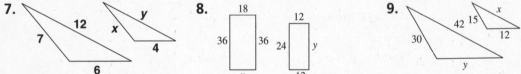

Additional Practice

1. a. Identify the three similar parallelograms in the figure at the right.

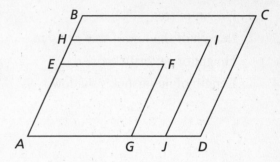

b. Name all sets of corresponding sides for the similar parallelograms you found.

c. Name all sets of corresponding angles for the similar parallelograms you found.

2. David is using the shadow method to estimate the heights of three trees in his schoolyard. For each set of data, make a diagram showing the tree, the meterstick and the shadows. Then determine the missing information.

a. Height of tree = ?

Length of shadow of tree = $\frac{9}{2}$ m

Height of meterstick = 1m

Length of meterstick's shadow = $\frac{1}{2}$ m

b. Height of tree = 6.5 m

Length of shadow of tree = ?

Height of meterstick = 1 m

Length of meterstick's shadow = $\frac{3}{4}$ m

Additional Practice (continued)

  c. Height of tree = 7.2 m

     Length of shadow of tree = 2.4 m

     Height of meterstick = 1m

     Length of meterstick's shadow = ?

  d. Height of tree = 7 m

     Length of shadow of tree = 3 m

     Height of meterstick = ?

     Length of meterstick's shadow = $\frac{3}{7}$ m

3. Charlotte is using the mirror method to find the heights of objects. Here are some of the measurements she recorded. Make a diagram for each situation, and determine the missing information.

  a. Height from the ground to Charlotte's eyes = 1.5 m

     Distance from center of mirror to Charlotte = 1.5 m

     Distance from center of mirror to shed = 2.5 m

     Height of the roof of the shed = ?

  b. Height from the ground to Charlotte's eyes = 1.5 m

     Distance from center of mirror to Charlotte = 0.5 m

     Distance from center of mirror to Charlotte's Great Dane = ?

     Height of Charlotte's Great Dane = 1 m

Additional Practice *(continued)*

4. Refer to the diagram below to answer parts (a)–(c).

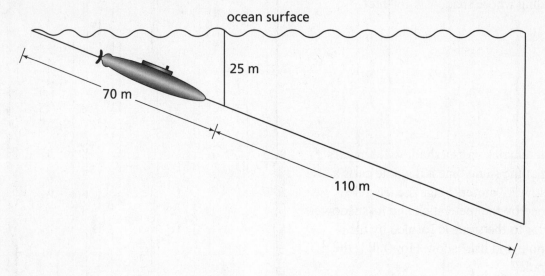

ocean surface

25 m

70 m

110 m

a. After traveling 70 meters in its dive, the submarine is at a depth of 25 meters. What will the submarine's depth be if it continues its dive for another 110 meters?

b. If the submarine continues on its present course and travels a total of 300 meters in its dive, what will the final depth of the submarine be?

c. If the submarine continues on its present course until a depth of 200 meters, how far will it have traveled?

Skill: Using Similarity

1. On a sunny day, if a 36-inch yardstick casts a 21-inch shadow, how tall is a building whose shadow is 168 feet?

2. A meter stick casts a shadow 1.4 meters long at the same time a flagpole casts a shadow 7.7 meters long. The triangle formed by the meterstick and its shadow is similar to the triangle formed by the flagpole and its shadow. How tall is the flagpole?

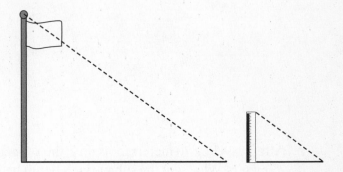

3. A rock show is being televised. The lead singer, who is 75 inches tall, is 15 inches tall on a TV monitor. The image of the bass player is 13 inches tall on the monitor. How tall is the bass player?

4. A 42-inch-long guitar is 10.5-feet-long on a stadium screen. A drum is 21 inches wide. How wide is the image on the stadium screen?

Additional Practice

1. a. According to the table, how long is a typical person's lifetime? Explain your reasoning.

Typical Person's Lifetime Activities

Activity	Number of Years
Sleeping	24.5
At work or school	13.5
Socializing	4.5
Watching TV	12
Reading	3
Eating	3
Bathing and grooming	1.75
Talking on the telephone	1
Miscellaneous activities*	9.5

* Such as housekeeping, shopping, waiting in lines, walking, driving, entertainment, and doing nothing

b. Does a typical person spend more years watching TV or sleeping? Write a ratio that compares these two amounts.

c. The number of years spent doing miscellaneous activities is about how many times the number of years spent socializing?

d. What percent of the total number of years in a lifetime are spent sleeping? What percent are spent at work or school?

e. About what fraction of a lifetime is spent watching TV and talking on the phone? What fraction is spent in miscellaneous activities?

f. Make an interesting comparison statement about the data in the table. Tell why you think your comparison is interesting.

Additional Practice (continued)

2. a. This table shows the typical weight of various parts of the body for an adult weighing 152 pounds. Estimate the percent of the total body weight for each part. Explain your reasoning.

Body Part	Weight (lb)
Head	10.5
Neck and Trunk	70.0
Arms	16.5
Hands	2
Legs	47.5
Feet	5.0

b. Make a circle graph that shows the percent of the total body weight for each body part.

c. The neck, trunk, and legs account for what total percent of the body weight?

3. a. Of the 756 students in Chad's middle school, 44% participate in sports, 29% play in the band, and 37% take the bus to school. How many students in Chad's middle school play in the band? Explain your reasoning.

b. How many students in Chad's middle school take the bus to school?

c. If you add up the percents of students who play sports, play in the band, and take the bus to school, you get 110%. Explain why the percents do not add to 100%.

Additional Practice (continued)

4. a. Of the students in Ms. Yadav's fourth-period math class, 16 are wearing athletic shoes, 10 are wearing boots, and 4 are wearing other kinds of shoes. What fraction of Ms. Yadav's students are wearing boots? Explain.

b. Suppose 1,006 students attend the middle school where Ms. Yadav teaches. Use your answer from part (a) to estimate the number of students who are wearing boots. Explain.

5. a. Use the table below. About what fraction of the total number of endangered species are found only in foreign countries?

Numbers of Endangered Species

	United States Only	United States and Foreign	Foreign Only
Animals	262	51	493
Plants	378	10	1
Total	640	61	494

b. How many times more endangered plant species are there in the United States than in foreign countries? Explain your reasoning.

c. About what percent of the total number of endangered animals lives only in the United States?

d. What is the ratio of Endangered Plants to Endangered Animals in the United States only? In foreign countries only?

e. What is the difference between the number of endangered animals in the United States and foreign countries and the number of endangered plants in the United States and foreign countries?

Name _____ Date _____ Class _____

Skill: Writing Ratios

Write three ratios that each diagram can represent.

1.

2.

The table at the right shows the results of a survey. Write a ratio for each comparison.

3. *Tacos* to *Pizza*

4. *Pizza* to *Tacos*

5. *Tacos* to the total

6. *Pizza* to the total

Which Meal Do You Want for the Party?

Tacos	Pizza
‖‖‖ ‖‖‖ ‖‖‖	‖‖‖ ‖‖‖ ‖‖‖ ‖

The table below shows the results when the seventh-grade classes were asked whether they wanted chicken or pasta served at their awards banquet. Use the table for Exercises 7–8.

Banquet Preferences

Room Number	Chicken	Pasta
201	10	12
202	8	17
203	16	10

7. In Room 201, what is the ratio of students who prefer chicken to students who prefer pasta?

8. Combine the totals for all three rooms. What is the ratio of the number of students who prefer pasta to the number of students who prefer chicken?

9. A bag contains 8 yellow marbles and 6 blue marbles. What number of yellow marbles can you add to the bag so that the ratio of yellow to blue marbles is 2 : 1?

42

Skill: Ratios and Fractions

Write each ratio in simplest form.

1. $\frac{2}{6}$

2. $3:21$

3. 16 to 20

4. $\frac{3}{30}$

5. 12 to 18

6. $81:27$

7. $\frac{6}{28}$

8. 49 to 14

Compare each pair of numbers. Use <, >, or =.

9. $\frac{7}{8}$ ☐ $\frac{3}{30}$

10. $\frac{4}{5}$ ☐ $\frac{1}{2}$

11. $\frac{6}{12}$ ☐ $\frac{4}{8}$

12. $\frac{7}{15}$ ☐ $\frac{11}{15}$

13. $\frac{4}{5}$ ☐ $\frac{6}{10}$

14. $\frac{7}{12}$ ☐ $\frac{2}{3}$

15. $\frac{8}{15}$ ☐ $\frac{1}{2}$

16. $\frac{10}{15}$ ☐ $\frac{8}{12}$

17. $\frac{4}{9}$ ☐ $\frac{7}{9}$

18. $\frac{2}{5}$ ☐ $\frac{3}{8}$

19. $\frac{1}{2}$ ☐ $\frac{11}{20}$

20. $\frac{7}{16}$ ☐ $\frac{1}{2}$

Additional Practice

1. **a.** Bill has a paper route. It takes him 50 minutes to deliver newspapers to his 40 customers. How long will it take Bill to complete his route if he adds 20 more customers in his neighborhood? Explain.

   b. Only 30 of Bill's 40 customers take the Sunday paper. About how long does it take Bill to deliver his papers on Sundays?

2. A micron is a metric unit of length. There are 1 million (1,000,000) microns in 1 meter.

   a. How many microns equal 1 centimeter? Explain.

   b. An object has a length of 2,911 microns. What is the length of the object in centimeters?

   c. An object has a width of 0.000351 meters. What is the width of the object in microns?

   d. Which metric unit—meters, centimeters, or microns—do you think is best to use to express the length of your pencil? Explain.

3. Betty and Derek are making punch for a class party. The directions on the liquid punch mix say to use 3 cups of mix for every 7 cups of water. Betty and Derek want to make enough punch so that each of the 25 people at the party can have 2 cups.

   a. How many cups of punch mix will Betty and Derek need to use? Explain.

   b. How many cups of water will Betty and Derek need to use?

   c. Betty and Derek want to put the punch in bowls that hold 20 cups each. How many bowls will they need?

Additional Practice (continued)

4. Use the diagrams below.

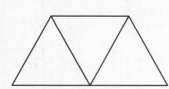 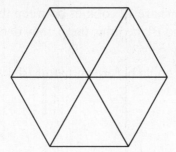 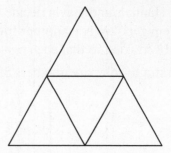

a. What is the ratio of the area of the trapezoid to the area of the hexagon? Explain your reasoning.

b. What is the ratio of the area of the large triangle to the area of the hexagon? Explain.

c. If the area of the hexagon is 24 square units, what is the area of the trapezoid? What is the area of the large triangle? Explain.

d. If the area of the trapezoid is 4 square units, what is the area of the large triangle?

5. Brice found three recipes for blueberry syrup. Of the ingredients, the ingredients only differed on the amount of blueberries and sugar:

　　Classic Blueberry syrup: 6 cups blueberries and 2 cups sugar

　　Homestyle Blueberry syrup: 2 cups blueberries and $\frac{1}{2}$ cup sugar

　　Country Blueberry syrup: 20 cups blueberries and 7 cups sugar

　Which recipe will be the sweetest? Explain.

Additional Practice (continued)

6. Gabrielle, Hannah, and Gavin decide to share 12 cookies between them, so each of them gets 4. When another friend Blake joins them, they decide to share the 12 cookies, so that each person gets 3.

   a. Use a ratio to compare numbers of people before and after Blake arrives.

   b. Use a ratio to compare the number of cookies in each share before and after Blake arrives.

   c. What do you notice about the ratios? Will this always be true?

7. At Louis Armstrong School, Ms. Turini's homeroom has 18 boys and 12 girls. Use ratios to describe the gender distribution of this class, by answering parts (a)–(d) in at least two equivalent ways.

   a. What is the ratio of boys to girls in Ms. Turini's homeroom?

   b. What is the ratio of girls to boys?

   c. What is the ratio of boys to students in the class?

   d. What is the ratio of students in the class to boys?

Skill: Equal Ratios

Find the value that makes the ratios equal.

1. 4 to 10, 2 to □

2. 51 to 18, □ to 6

3. $\frac{12}{12}, \frac{□}{20}$

4. $\frac{15}{7}, \frac{□}{21}$

5. $\frac{28}{56}, \frac{□}{14}$

6. 36 to 12, □ to 1

Find the value that makes each sentence correct.

7. $\frac{4}{5} = \frac{□}{15}$

8. $\frac{8}{□} = \frac{4}{15}$

9. $\frac{3}{2} = \frac{21}{□}$

10. $\frac{□}{5} = \frac{32}{20}$

11. $\frac{7}{8} = \frac{□}{32}$

12. $\frac{5}{4} = \frac{15}{□}$

13. 8 to 12 = □ to 6

14. 9 : 12 = 3 : □

Additional Practice

1. Among American physicians, more are male than female. However, the ratio varies in different age groups. Use the table to answer parts (a)–(d).

American Physicians, Beginning of 1998

	< 35	35–44	45–54	55–64
Male	84,445	152,210	142,314	92,260
Female	49,395	61,192	33,180	12,022

Source: AMA cited in *The World Almanac and Book of Facts, 1999,* page 881.

Approximate each of the following ratios in three equivalent forms. Begin by rounding the given data to the nearest 5,000 to form the first ratios.

The ratio of male to female doctors in the

a. under 35 age group;   **b.** 35–44 age group;

c. 45–54 age group;   **d.** 55–64 age group.

2. Use the approximate ratio data on male and female physicians in example 1 to answer these questions. Express each answer in two equivalent forms—one a fraction and one a percent.

What fraction of physicians are females in the

a. under 35 years age group?   **b.** 35–44 age group?

c. 45–54 age group?   **d.** 55–64 age group?

3. Josh jogs an average of 8 miles per week for three weeks.

a. At this rate, how many miles will he jog in 52 weeks?

b. How many miles will he need to jog during the fourth week to bring his four-week average to 10 miles per week?

Additional Practice (continued)

4. Tony can type at a constant rate of 55 words per minute.

   a. Write an equation for the number of words W Tony can type in T minutes.

   b. How many words can Tony type in 20 minutes?

   c. If Tony has a half hour to type a 1,600-word essay, will he have time to type the entire essay? Explain your reasoning.

5. The following table shows caffeine content of 12-ounce cans for five popular soft drinks.

Caffeine Content in Milligrams

	12-Ounce Can	20-Ounce Bottle
Diet Sun Drop	69	
Mountain Dew	55	
Dr. Pepper	41	
Pepsi Cola	38	
Coca-Cola	34	
Barq's Root Beer	22	

Source: National Soft Drink Associates as given in "Soft Drinks Hard Facts"
The Washington Post/Health/February 27, 2001, page 12.

   a. Complete entries in the column giving caffeine content of 20-ounce bottles for each soft drink.

   b. Compare caffeine content in the soft drinks above. In each case, use the exact data first. Then give a simpler ratio that is exactly or nearly equivalent to the first.

   i. Diet Sun Drop to Barq's Root Beer

   ii. Mountain Dew to Dr. Pepper

   iii. Mountain Dew to Coca Cola

Additional Practice *(continued)*

6. When people predict the chances that some athlete, team, racehorse, or car will win a competition, they often express their guess as a statement about the "odds against" winning. For example, they might predict that odds on the Yankees winning the World Series are 7 to 2, meaning that the probability of that event is $\frac{2}{9}$. A horse that leaves the starting gate with odds 11 to 5 is predicted to have probability $\frac{5}{16}$ of winning.

   a. What is the probability that a team will win a game if the reported odds are 6 to 4? 8 to 5? 3 to 5? A to B?

   b. What simpler odds statements could be given if the reported odds are 12 to 9? 8 to 2? 15 to 6?

   c. What odds would be stated if the probability of winning a contest is $\frac{2}{3}$? $\frac{5}{8}$? $\frac{4}{13}$? $\frac{A}{B}$?

7. A veterinarian's clinic has a patient load of 150 cats and dogs. The ratio of cats to dogs is 4 to 8. How many patients are cats and how many are dogs? Explain your reasoning.

8. On a map, 1 centimeter = 50 kilometers. What is the actual distance between two towns that are 3.5 centimeters apart on the map? Explain your reasoning.

Additional Practice (continued)

9. The numbers in the table are projections based on a 1993 survey of 10,000 households. The survey counted anyone 7 years old or older who participated in an activity more than once per year. Be ready to explain your strategies for answering parts (a)–(d).

Participation in Sports Activities in the United States

Activity	Males	Females	Ages 12–17	Ages 55–64
Bicycle	24,562,000	23,357,000	8,794,000	2,030,000
Camping	23,165,000	19,533,000	5,336,000	2,355,000
Exercise walking	21,054,000	43,373,000	2,816,000	7,782,000
Fishing	30,449,000	14,885,000	4,945,000	3,156,000
Swimming	27,713,000	33,640,000	10,874,000	2,756,000
Total in group	111,851,000	118,555,000	21,304,000	20,922,000

Source: National Sporting Goods Association, as found in the *Statistical Abstract of the United States 1995,* Published by the Bureau of the Census, Washington DC, p. 260.

a. Why don't the numbers in the columns add to the given totals?

b. Is it fair to say that exercise walking is about twice as popular among females as among males? Use fractions, ratios, percents, or differences to support or contradict that claim.

c. Is it fair to say that swimming is about 4 times as popular among young people (ages 12–17) as among older people (ages 55–64)? Use fractions, ratios, percents, or differences to support or contradict that claim.

d. Can you compare the participation of teenage boys in these activities to the participation of older-adult women by using the data in the table?

e. The U.S. population in 1993 was about 258 million. In 2000 it was about 281 million. What projections of male and female participants in the five popular sports would you make for 2000?

Skill: Finding and Using Rates

Write the unit rate for each situation.

1. travel 250 miles in 5 hours

2. earn $75.20 in 8 hours

3. read 80 pages in 2 hours

4. type 8,580 words in 2 hours 45 minutes

5. manufacture 2,488 parts in 8 hours

6. 50 copies of a book on 2 shelves

7. $30 for 6 books

8. 24 points in 3 games

Find each unit price. Then determine the better buy.

9. paper: 100 sheets for $0.99
         500 sheets for $4.29

10. peanuts: 1 pound for $1.29
          12 ounces for $0.95

11. crackers: 15 ounces for $1.79
          12 ounces for $1.49

12. apples: 3 pounds for $1.89
          5 pounds for $2.49

13. mechanical pencils: 4 for $1.25
                25 for $5.69

14. bagels: 4 for $0.89
          6 for $1.39

Skill: Finding and Using Rates (continued)

15. a. Yolanda and Yoko ran in a 100-yd dash. When Yolanda crossed the finish line in 15 seconds, Yoko was 10 yards behind her. The girls then repeated the race, with Yolanda starting 10 yards behind the starting line. If each girl ran at the same rate as before, who won the race? By how many yards?

   b. Assume the girls run at the same rate as before. How far behind the starting line should Yolanda be in order for the two to finish in a tie?

16. During the breaststroke competitions of a recent Olympics, Nelson Diebel swam 100 meters in 62 seconds, and Mike Bowerman swam 200 meters in 130 seconds. Who swam at a faster rate?

17. During a vacation, the Vasquez family traveled 174 miles in 3 hours on Monday, and 290 miles in 5 hours on Tuesday. Write an equation relating miles *m* traveled to hours *h*.

Additional Practice

1. Kyle has maintained a consistent batting average of 0.350 on the Metropolis Middle School baseball team during the first half of the season. Assuming his batting average stays the same for the rest of the season, write and solve proportions to answer parts (a)–(d).

   a. How many hits will Kyle make in his next 20 times at bat?

   b. How many hits will Kyle make in his next 35 times at bat?

   c. How many times at bat will it take Kyle to make 10 hits?

   d. How many times at bat will it take Kyle to make 18 hits?

2. In a home-run derby contest after the little league baseball session had ended, Calvin hit 4 homeruns out of his 12 hits. Suppose Calvin's success rate stays about the same for his next 100 hits. Write and solve proportions to answer parts (a)–(d).

   a. About how many homeruns will Calvin make out of his next 48 hits?

   b. About how many homeruns will Calvin make out of his next 84 hits?

   c. About how many hits will it take for Calvin to hit 8 more homeruns?

   d. About how many hits will it take for him to make 36 more homeruns?

Additional Practice (continued)

3. Find the value of x that makes the two ratios equivalent.

   a. 4 to 7 and x to 63

   b. 4 to 7 and x to 87.15

   c. 12 to x and 4 to 117

   d. 12 to x and 15 to 45

   e. 2 to 3 and 7 to x

   f. 23 to 115 and x to 15

4. The Elsie Dairy uses a machine that fills 28 cartons of milk an hour.

   a. How many cartons will be filled in 6.5 hours?

   b. How long will it take to fill 343 cartons?

   c. If the machine ran continuously for 10 days, how many cartons would it fill?

   d. Write an equation that expresses the relationship between the number of cartons C and the number of hours H.

Skill: Solving Proportions

Solve each proportion for the missing value.

1. $\frac{k}{8} = \frac{14}{4}$

2. $\frac{u}{3} = \frac{10}{5}$

3. $\frac{14}{6} = \frac{d}{15}$

4. $\frac{5}{1} = \frac{m}{4}$

5. $\frac{36}{32} = \frac{n}{8}$

6. $\frac{5}{30} = \frac{1}{x}$

7. $\frac{t}{4} = \frac{5}{10}$

8. $\frac{9}{2} = \frac{v}{4}$

9. $\frac{x}{10} = \frac{6}{4}$

10. $\frac{8}{12} = \frac{2}{b}$

11. $\frac{v}{15} = \frac{4}{6}$

12. $\frac{3}{18} = \frac{2}{s}$

Estimate the solution of each proportion.

13. $\frac{m}{25} = \frac{16}{98}$

14. $\frac{7}{3} = \frac{52}{n}$

15. $\frac{30}{5.9} = \frac{k}{10}$

16. $\frac{2.8}{j} = \frac{1.3}{2.71}$

17. $\frac{y}{12} = \frac{2.89}{4.23}$

18. $\frac{5}{8} = \frac{b}{63}$

Skill: Solving Proportions (continued)

Comparing and Scaling

19. A contractor estimates it will cost $2,400 to build a deck to a customer's specifications. How much would it cost to build five more identical decks?

20. A recipe requires 3 cups of flour to make 27 dinner rolls. How much flour is needed to make 9 rolls?

21. Mandy runs 4 kilometers in 18 minutes. She plans to run in a 15-kilometer race. How long will it take her to complete the race?

22. Ken's new car can go 26 miles per gallon of gasoline. The car's gasoline tank holds 14 gallons. How far will he be able to go on a full tank?

23. Eleanor can complete two skirts in 15 days. How long will it take her to complete eight skirts?

24. Three eggs are required to make two dozen muffins. How many eggs are needed to make 12 dozen muffins?

Additional Practice

1. On a chip board, what value is represented by each set of chips?
   (B = black, R = red)

   a. 5 B, 3 R   **b.** 5 B, 4 R   **c.** 5 B, 5 R   **d.** 5 B, 6 R

   e. 3 B, 5 R   **f.** 4 B, 5 R   **g.** 5 B, 5 R   **h.** 6 B, 5 R

2. On a chip board, what value is represented by each set of chips?
   (B = black, R = red)

   a. 5 B, 5 R   **b.** 12 B, 12 R   **c.** 44 B, 44 R   **d.** 113 B, 113 R

   e. What pattern do you see?

3. Write 3 different combinations of chips that show each value:

   a. 2   **b.** ⁻4   **c.** 0   **d.** ⁻18

4. Sarah added 7 pairs of black and red chips to her chip board. How did the value change? Explain.

5. Sam added 4 black and 7 red chips to his chip board. How did the value change? Explain.

58

Additional Practice (continued)

The team in Exercises 6–10 each answered five questions. The score for four of the questions and the final score are given for each team. Give the point value of the fifth question and tell whether the team answered it correctly.

6. The Smarts answered a 150-point question correctly, a 200-point question correctly, a 50-point question incorrectly, and a 250-point question incorrectly. Their final score was 250 points.

7. The Brains answered a 150-point question incorrectly, a 200-point question correctly, a 150-point question correctly, and a 50-point question incorrectly. Their final score was 0 points.

8. The Minds answered a 200-point question incorrectly, a 50-point question correctly, a 100-point question incorrectly, and a 250-point question correctly. Their final score was 150 points.

9. The MegaBrains answered a 150-point question correctly, a 100-point question correctly, a 100-point question incorrectly, and a 250-point question correctly. Their final score was 150 points.

10. The SoSmarts answered a 50-point question incorrectly, a 150-point question correctly, a 100-point question incorrectly, and a 50-point question correctly. Their final score was ⁻200 points.

Additional Practice (continued)

For Exercises 11–15, find two numbers that meet the given conditions.

11. Both numbers are less than 10.
The distance between the two numbers on the number line is 14.

12. Both numbers are greater than ⁻15 and less than 5.
One number is 6 greater than the other number.

13. One number is ⁻35.
The distance between the two numbers on the number line is 20.

14. The numbers are opposites.
The distance between the two numbers on the number line is 18.

15. The first number is the opposite of ⁻17.
The second number is less than the first number.
The distance between the two numbers on the number line is 9.

For Exercises 16–20, use the following information: At 10:00 A.M. on a winter day in Fairbanks, Alaska, the temperature was ⁻12°F. Find the temperature after each of the following temperature changes.

16. Between 10:00 A.M. and noon, the temperature rose 10°F.

17. Between noon and 3:00 P.M., the temperature rose 15°F.

18. Between 3:00 P.M. and 6:00 P.M., the temperature dropped 13°F.

19. Between 6:00 P.M. and 9:00 P.M., the temperature dropped 26°F.

20. Between 9:00 P.M. and midnight, the temperature changed by ⁻19°F.

Name _____ Date _____ Class _____

Additional Practice (continued)

For Exercises 21–25, use the sketch below, which shows a submarine cruising at a depth of 100 meters. In your answers, express an increase in depth as a positive number and a decrease as a negative number.

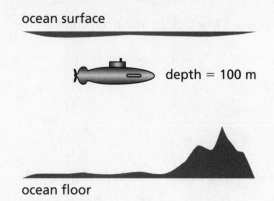

ocean surface

depth = 100 m

ocean floor

21. If the submarine moves from its depth of 100 meters to a depth of 75 meters, what is the change in its depth?

22. If the submarine dives from a depth of 100 meters to a depth of 180 meters, what is the change in its depth?

23. If the submarine surfaces from a depth of 180 meters, what is the change in its depth?

24. The submarine is cruising at a depth of 50 meters, then dives 75 meters, then ascends (moves in the direction of the surface) 60 meters, and then dives 45 meters. What is the submarine's final depth?

25. The submarine is cruising at a depth of 65 meters. Then it dives 15 meters, ascends 55 meters, and then dives 75 meters. At this final position, what is the change in depth from its initial position?

Additional Practice (continued)

For Exercises 26–30, describe the chips that were on the chip board before the given action took place. Then write an additional sentence that describes the value of the original board, the value of the chips that are added, and the new value of the board.

26. 7 black chips are added. Now there are 8 black chips and 3 red chips on the board.

27. 5 red chips are added. Now there are 8 black chips and 12 red chips on the board.

28. 2 black chips and 2 red chips are added. Now there are 5 black chips and 3 red chips on the board.

29. 5 black chips and 8 red chips are added. Now there are 7 black chips and 8 red chips on the board.

30. 6 black chips and 8 red chips are added. Now there are 6 black chips and 11 red chips on the board.

Skill: Integers

Name the integer represented by each point on the number line.

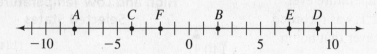

1. A **2.** B **3.** C **4.** D **5.** E **6.** F

Insert <, >, or = to make a true sentence.

7. $-8 \ \square \ 8$ **8.** $4 \ \square \ -4$ **9.** $-8 \ \square \ 0$

10. $-6 \ \square \ -2$ **11.** $-1 \ \square \ -3$ **12.** $|-4| \ \square \ 0$

Graph each integer and its opposite on the number line.

13. -9 **14.** 5

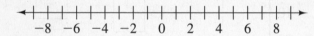 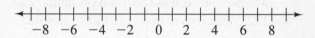

15. 6 **16.** 7

 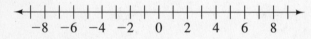 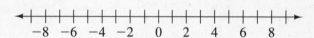

17. 8 **18.** -2

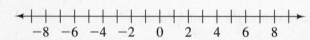 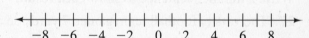

Order the integers in each set from least to greatest.

19. $0, -5, 5, -15, 15, 25, -25$ **20.** $6, -4, -8, 3, 1, -2, 7$

21. $27, -10, -6, -18, 3, 9, -8$ **22.** $-3, -7, 7, 4, -9, -4, -1$

Skill: Integers (continued)

Use the information in the graph at the right for Exercises 23–26.

23. The highest outdoor temperature ever recorded in Nevada, 122°F, was recorded on June 23, 1954. Was it ever that hot in Idaho? Explain.

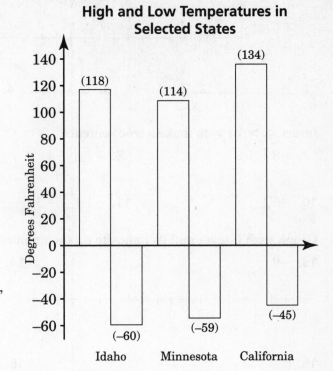

High and Low Temperatures in Selected States

24. Which state had a recorded high temperature of 134°F?

25. The lowest temperature ever recorded in Maine, −48°F, was recorded on January 17, 1925. Was it ever that cold in Minnesota? Explain.

26. Which state on the graph had a recorded low temperature of 60°F below zero?

Write a number sentence to show each result.

27. The varsity football team gained 7 yards on one play and then lost 4 yards.

28. The airplane descended 140 feet and then rose 112 feet.

29. The squirrel climbed 18 inches up a tree, slipped back 4 inches, and then climbed up 12 inches more.

30. The temperature was 72°F at noon. At midnight a cold front moved in, dropping the temperature 12°F.

Additional Practice

1. An amount paid to a business for goods or services is a *credit,* and an amount the business pays for goods, services, or debts is a *debit.* The chart below shows the total monthly credits and debits for the student store for the first six months of the school year.

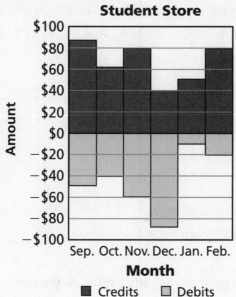

Student Store

Credits   Debits

a. What is the total of the credits for September through February?

b. What is the total of the debits for September through February?

c. Did the store make or lose money over this time period? Explain your reasoning.

d. Adding the credits and debits gives the profit or loss for a given period of time. Tell which months the store showed a loss and which months the store showed a profit. Explain.

For Exercises 2–4, explain how you could use chips and a chip board to find the difference. Then, find the difference.

2. $^-8 - 5$ 3. $3 - 9$ 4. $^-6 - ^-12$

Additional Practice (continued)

Write both an addition sentence and a subtraction sentence to represent what is shown on the number line.

5.

6.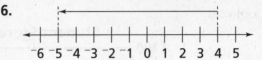

7. A chip board has 10 red chips and 10 black chips.

   a. What value is represented by this board?

   b. If 2 red chips and 2 black chips are removed, what value do the remaining chips represent?

   c. If 20 red chips and 20 black chips are added, what value do the chips represent?

Find the missing value.

8. $\square + 5 = 7$

9. $5 + \square = {}^-3$

10. $\square + {}^-3 = {}^-9$

11. $7 - \square = 3$

12. $\square - 10 = {}^-6$

13. $7 - \square = 12$

14. ${}^-6 - \square = 7$

15. ${}^-3.4 - \square = {}^-5.6$

16. $\frac{2}{3} - \square = 1$

17. $\square - 12 = {}^-5$

18. ${}^-4.5 - \frac{9}{2} = \square$

19. $3\frac{2}{5} + \square = \frac{2}{5}$

20. $\square + 7.6 = 3\frac{3}{5}$

21. $\square - {}^-7.8 = 0$

22. $\square + \frac{-93}{10} = 10$

Additional Practice (continued)

23. Decide whether the statement is always true, sometimes true, or always false. Explain your reasoning.

    a. If a positive integer is subtracted from a negative integer, the difference is a negative integer.

    b. If a positive integer is subtracted from a positive integer, the difference is a positive integer.

24. Write a complete fact family for each of the following:

    a. $^-5 + {}^+2 = {}^-3$ **b.** $^-4 + {}^-6 = {}^-10$

    b. $^+0.7 + {}^+0.3 = {}^+1.0$ **d.** $^-3.1 + {}^-1.1 = {}^-4.4$

25. Chris said that the fact family for $^-2 + {}^+7 = {}^+5$ should have facts:

    $^-2 + {}^+7 = {}^+5$ $^+5 = {}^-2 + {}^+7$

    $^+5 - {}^-2 = {}^+7$ and $^+7 = {}^+5 - {}^-2$

    $^+5 - {}^+7 = {}^-2$ $^-2 = {}^+5 - {}^+7$

Do you agree? Explain.

Additional Practice (continued)

For Exercises 26–30, show the addition on a number line, and give the sum.

26. $^+8 + {}^-8$

27. $^-2 + {}^-5 + {}^-4$

28. $^+8 + {}^-9 + {}^-2$

29. $^-8 + {}^+8 + {}^-3$

30. $^-10 + {}^+5 + {}^+4 + 1$

For Exercises 31–34, write the addition sentence illustrated by each figure.

31.

32.

33.

34.

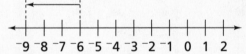

35. Bill said that $^-7 - {}^+4$ and $^+7 + {}^-10$ both represent the same number.

 a. Draw a chip board to represent each combination.

 b. Do both combinations of chips represent the same number? Explain your reasoning.

Additional Practice

36. Tell which one of the following sums is different from the others, and explain your reasoning: $^-3 + {}^+5$, $^+8 + {}^-5$, $^+7 + {}^-5$, and $^+12 + {}^-10$.

37. On Friday, Anessa has $5. Over the weekend, she buys a granola bar for $0.75, sees a movie for $3.50, gets $2 from her brother who is repaying a loan, and then spends $1.25 at the arcade. How much money does Anessa have at the end of the weekend?

38. Scientists sometimes use a temperature scale called the Kelvin scale. The relationship between the Kelvin temperature scale and the Celsius temperature scale is expressed by the equation $K = C + 273$ where K is degrees Kelvin and C is degrees Celsius.

   a. What is $^-45°C$ in degrees Kelvin?

   b. What is $71°K$ in degrees Celsius?

   c. If the temperature of a substance ranges from $102°K$ to $230°K$, what is the temperature range in degrees Celsius?

Skill: Adding Integers

Accentuate the Negative

Simplify each expression.

1. $-2 + (-3)$

2. $8 - 7 + 4$

3. $8 + (-5)$

4. $15 + (-3)$

5. $-16 + 8$

6. $7 + (-10)$

7. $-9 + (-5)$

8. $-12 + 14$

9. $8 + 7$

10. $9 + (-4)$

11. $-6 + (-8)$

12. $8 + (-14)$

13. $9 + (-17)$

14. $-15 + (-11)$

15. $-23 + 18$

16. $-19 + 16$

17. $27 + 34$

18. $-8 + (-17)$

19. $19 + (-8)$

20. $23 + (-31)$

Skill: Subtracting Integers

Find each difference.

1. $9 - 26$

2. $-4 - 15$

3. $21 - (-7)$

4. $27 - (-16)$

5. $-16 - (-43)$

6. $47 - 19$

7. $-156 - 98$

8. $-192 - 47$

9. $0 - (-51)$

10. $-63 - 89$

11. $-12 - (-21)$

12. $92 - (-16)$

13. $72 - 15$

14. $-86 - (-19)$

15. $17 - (-46)$

16. $-78 - (-53)$

17. $-19 - (-12)$

18. $-16 - (-21)$

19. $27 - 19$

20. $-14 - 27$

Skill: Adding and Subtracting Rational Numbers

Find each sum or difference as a mixed number or fraction in simplest form.

1. $\frac{3}{4} + \frac{7}{8}$

2. $-1\frac{1}{6} + 2\frac{2}{3}$

3. $4\frac{1}{2} - 7\frac{7}{8}$

4. $-3\frac{5}{6} - \left(4\frac{1}{12}\right)$

5. $\frac{5}{18} + \frac{7}{12}$

6. $-4\frac{7}{20} + 3\frac{9}{10}$

7. $5\frac{8}{21} - \left(-3\frac{1}{7}\right)$

8. $1\frac{19}{24} + 2\frac{23}{20}$

9. $3\frac{16}{25} - 4\frac{7}{20}$

Write each answer as a fraction or mixed number in simplest form.

10. $14.6 + \left(-3\frac{1}{5}\right)$

11. $-7\frac{3}{4} + 4.125$

12. $5.75 + \left(-2\frac{1}{8}\right)$

Skill: Coordinate Graphing

Name the point with the given coordinates.

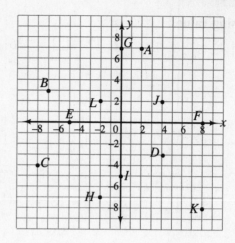

1. $(-2, 2)$

2. $(8, 0)$

3. $(4, -3)$

4. $(-7, 3)$

5. $(0, -5)$

6. $(-8, -4)$

Write the coordinates of each point.

7. E

8. A

9. H

10. K

11. G

12. J

Identify the quadrant in which each point lies.

13. $(-4, 3)$

14. $(7, 21)$

15. $(5, -8)$

16. $(-2, -7)$

Additional Practice

Find the missing value.

1. $\square \times 8 = 56$

2. $12 \times \square = {}^{-}36$

3. $\square \times {}^{-}10 = 90$

4. $7 \times \square = {}^{-}147$

5. $\square \div 18 = {}^{-}54$

6. $64 \div \square = 8$

7. ${}^{-}192 \div \square = 16$

8. ${}^{-}99.99 \div \square = {}^{-}3.03$

9. $\frac{2}{3} \times \square = \frac{10}{24}$

10. $\square \times 13 = {}^{-}169$

11. ${}^{-}234 \div 12.5 = \square$

12. $3\frac{1}{5} \div \square = {}^{-}8$

13. $\square \times {}^{-}7.6 = 67.64$

14. $\square \div {}^{-}77.8 = 1$

15. $\square \div \frac{{}^{-}93}{10} = 10$

Additional Practice (continued)

16. Write a complete fact family for each of the following:

a. $^-5 \times {}^+2 = {}^-10$ **b.** $^-4 \times {}^-6 = {}^+24$

c. $^+0.6 \div {}^-0.3 = {}^-2$ **d.** $^-32 \div {}^-8 = {}^+4$

17. For the Number Line Game there are three number cubes marked as shown:

  blue number cube: +, +, +, −, −, −

  red number cube: $^-1, {}^-2, {}^-3, {}^-4, {}^-5, {}^-6$

  green number cube: $^+1, {}^+2, {}^+3, {}^+4, {}^+5, {}^+6$

You start with a cumulative total of 0. On each turn, you roll the cube, multiply the numbers, and add or subtract the product to your cumulative total. The winner is the person whose cumulative total is closest to 0 after each player has taken 5 turns.

Here are the rolls for Juan, Shandra, and Kasper. Who won?

Juan	Shandra	Kasper
+, $^-2$, $^+3$	+, $^-1$, $^+2$	−, $^-6$, $^+1$
+, $^-4$, $^+1$	−, $^-5$, $^+2$	−, $^-1$, $^+4$
−, $^-2$, $^+2$	−, $^-3$, $^+4$	+, $^-1$, $^+4$
+, $^-3$, $^+6$	−, $^-3$, $^+5$	+, $^-1$, $^+5$
−, $^-2$, $^+6$	+, $^-6$, $^+6$	+, $^-4$, $^+4$

Skill: Multiplying Integers

Multiply.

1. 7×8

2. -5×7

3. $4 \times (-8)$

4. $-8 \times (-2)$

5. $11 \times (-6)$

6. -7×6

7. $-8 \times (-8)$

8. 10×4

9. 21×13

10. -15×12

11. $-25 \times (-14)$

12. $10 \times (-25)$

For Exercises 13–18, find the missing number.

13. $3 \times \square = -6$

14. $4 \times \square = -4$

15. $\square \times (24) = -8$

16. $-3 \times \square = 9$

17. $-9 \times (-2) = \square$

18. $\square \times (-2) = -18$

19. Your teacher purchases 24 pastries for a class celebration, at $2 each. What integer expresses the amount he paid?

20. Temperatures have been falling steadily at 5°F each day. What integer expresses the change in temperature in degrees 7 days from today?

21. A submarine starts at the surface of the Pacific Ocean and descends 60 feet every hour. What integer expresses the submarine's depth in feet after 6 hours?

22. A skydiver falls at approximately 10 meters per second. Write a number sentence to express how many meters he will fall in 40 seconds.

Skill: Dividing Integers

Divide.

1. $14 \div 7$

2. $21 \div (-3)$

3. $-15 \div 5$

4. $-27 \div (-9)$

5. $45 \div (-9)$

6. $-42 \div 6$

7. $-105 \div (-15)$

8. $63 \div (-9)$

9. $108 \div 6$

10. $-204 \div 17$

11. $240 \div (-15)$

12. $-252 \div (-12)$

Find each product or quotient.

13. $\frac{-36}{9}$

14. $\frac{-52}{-4}$

15. $(-5) \cdot (-20)$

16. $\frac{-63}{-9}$

17. $(-15) \cdot (2)$

18. $\frac{22}{-2}$

19. $(13) \cdot (-6)$

20. $\frac{-100}{-5}$

21. $(-60) \cdot (-3)$

For Exercises 22 and 23, represent each pattern of change with an integer.

22. spends $300 in 5 days

23. runs 800 feet in 4 minutes

24. Juan's baseball card collection was worth $800. Over the last 5 years, the collection decreased $300 in value. What integer represents the average decrease in value each year?

25. Florence purchased stock for $20 per share. After 6 days, the stock is worth $32 per share. What integer represents the average increase in stock value each day?

Skill: Multiplying and Dividing Rational Numbers

Use the algorithms you developed to find each value.

1. $-\frac{1}{6} \cdot 2\frac{3}{4}$

2. $\frac{3}{16} \div \left(-\frac{1}{8}\right)$

3. $-\frac{31}{56} \cdot (-8)$

4. $-5\frac{7}{12} \div 12$

5. $-8 \div \frac{1}{4}$

6. $-3\frac{1}{6} \div \left(-2\frac{1}{12}\right)$

7. $8\frac{3}{4} \cdot 3\frac{7}{8}$

8. $-\frac{11}{12} \div \frac{5}{6}$

9. $4\frac{9}{28} \cdot (-7)$

10. $-1\frac{1}{15} \div 15$

11. $-3 \div \frac{3}{4}$

12. $-2\frac{7}{8} \div 3\frac{3}{4}$

13. $-\frac{23}{24} \cdot (-8)$

14. $\frac{7}{8} \cdot \left(-\frac{2}{7}\right)$

15. $-7 \div \frac{1}{9}$

Additional Practice

1. Find each missing value.

a. $13 - (8 - 2) = 13 - 8 - \square$

b. $-6 - (5 - 3) = -6 - 5 - \square$

c. $12 - (6 - -1) = 12 - 6 - \square$

d. $-22 - (-11 - -4) = -22 - -11 - \square$

e. What pattern do you see?

2. Find the correct result for each of the following.

a. $-5 \times 7 + 10 \div 2$

b. $(2 + 4)^2 \times 5 - 2$

c. $3\frac{2}{5} \times 2\frac{1}{2} - 5^3 + 10$

d. $6 \times (3 - 5)^2 + 8$

e. $-6 \times (7 - (-4 + 2))$

f. $-9 \times 8 \div 2^3 + -5$

3. Find the answers to the following expressions.

a. $5 \times 8 \div 2 \div 2$

b. $3 + -5 \times 4 - 2$

c. $5 \times 2 \times -3 + -12 \div 6$

d. $-4 \times (3 + -10) - 3^2$

e. $(8 - 20) \div 2^2 - 5 \times -3$

f. $20 - (60 \div (-2 \times 30) - 8) \times 2^2$

g. $12 - 8 + 4 - 3$

h. $4^2 + \frac{-10}{2} + 13$

4. Find each missing value.

a. $4 \times 8 + 4 \times 22 = 4 \times \square$

b. $-12 \times 43 + -12 \times -3 = -12 \times \square$

c. $-6 \times \square = -6 \times 15 + -6 \times -5$

d. $-0.4 \times \square = -0.4 \times -0.7 + -0.4 \times -0.3$

Additional Practice (continued)

5. Find each missing value.

a. $2 \times (-7 + 4) = 2 \times -7 + 2 \times 4 = \underline{} + \underline{} = \underline{}$

b. $1 \times (-7 + 4) = \underline{} \times -7 + \underline{} \times 4 = \underline{} + \underline{} = \underline{}$

c. $0 \times (-7 + 4) = \underline{} \times -7 + \underline{} \times 4 = \underline{} + \underline{} = \underline{}$

d. $-1 \times (-7 + 4) = \underline{} \times -7 + \underline{} \times 4 = \underline{} + \underline{} = \underline{}$

e. $-2 \times (-7 + 4) = \underline{} \times -7 + \underline{} \times 4 = \underline{} + \underline{} = \underline{}$

f. What patterns do you see? Explain your thinking.

6. Fill in the missing parts to make the sentences true.

a. $8 \times (6 + 4) = (8 \times \underline{}) + (8 \times 4)$

b. $7 \times (x + 3) = (7 \times \underline{}) + (\underline{} \times 3)$

c. $(-9 \times 5) + (\underline{} \times 7) = -9 \times (\underline{} + 7)$

d. $(x \times 4) + (x \times 5) = \underline{} \times (4 + 5)$

e. $8x + 12x = x \times (\underline{} + \underline{})$

7. Use the Distributive Property to write an expression equal to each of the following:

a. $-3 \cdot (4 + -7)$

b. $(-5 \cdot 3) - (-5 \cdot -13)$

c. $10 \cdot (-3 + 5)$

d. $(-12x) + (4x)$

e. $2 \cdot (2 - -4)$

f. $(x) - (4x)$

Skill: Order of Operations With Integers

Find the value of each expression.

1. $(8 + 2) \times 9$ **2.** $5 - 1 \div 4$ **3.** $(6 + 3) \div 18$ **4.** $80 - 6 \times 7$

5. $4 \times 6 + 3$ **6.** $4 \times (6 + 3)$ **7.** $35 - 6 \times 5$ **8.** $8 \div 3 + 6$

9. $(-4)^2 + 10 \cdot 2$ **10.** $-4^2 + 10 \cdot 2$ **11.** $(5 \cdot 3)^2 + 8$

12. $5 \cdot 3^2 + 8$ **13.** $9 + (7 - 4)^2$ **14.** $-9 + 7 - 4^2$

15. $(-6)^2 + 3^3 - 7$ **16.** $-6^2 + 3^3 - 7$ **17.** $2^3 + (8 - 5) \cdot 4 - 5^2$

18. $(2^3 + 8) - 5 \cdot 4 - 5^2$ **19.** $2^3 \cdot 3 - 5 \cdot 5^2 + 8$ **20.** $2^3 \cdot 3 - 5(5^2 + 8)$

Skill: Properties of Operations

Find the missing part(s) to make each sentence true.

1. $5(9 + 6) = 5\,(\square) + 5\,(\square)$

2. $4(9.7 - 8.1) = \square(9.7) - \square(8.1)$

3. $\square(3.8) = 9(4) - 9(\square)$

4. $\square(17.1 + 12.6) = 6(17.1) + 6(12.6)$

Copy and place parentheses to make each statement true.

5. $6 + 6 \div 6 \times 6 + 6 = 24$

6. $6 \times 6 + 6 \times 6 - 6 = 426$

7. $6 + 6 \div 6 \times 6 - 6 = 0$

8. $6 - 6 \times 6 + 6 \div 6 = 1$

9. $6 + 6 \div 6 + 6 \times 6 = 6$

10. $6 - 6 \div 6 \times 6 + 6 = 0$

Multiply each expression.

11. $6(h - 4)$

12. $(p + 3)5$

13. $-3(x + 8)$

14. $(4 - y)(-9)$

15. $2(7n - 11)$

16. $-10(-a + 5)$

Additional Practice

For Exercises 1–3, refer to this table.

Cycling time (hours)	Distance (miles)		
	Francine	Geraldo	Jennifer
0	0	0	0
1	4.5	6	7.5
2	9	12	15
3	13.5	18	22.5
4	18	24	30

1. a. How fast did each person travel for the first four hours? Explain.

   b. Assume that each person continued at this rate. Find the distance each person traveled in 6 hours.

2. a. Graph the time and distance for all three people on the same coordinate axes.

   b. Use the graphs to find the distance each person traveled in 2.5 hours.

   c. Use the graphs to find the time it took each person to travel 70 miles.

   d. How does the rate at which each person rides affect the graphs?

3. a. For each rider, write an equation you can use to calculate the distance traveled after a given number of hours.

   b. Describe how you could use your equations to calculate the distance each person traveled in 2.5 hours.

   c. How does each person's biking rate show up in the equation?

4. Stilton was also on the bike trip. The distance he traveled after t hours is represented by $d = 7.25t$.

   a. At what rate of speed is Stilton traveling?

   b. If you were to put the graph of Stilton's distance and time on the same set of axes as the graphs for Francine, Geraldo, and Jennifer of the previous page, how would it compare to the other three graphs?

5. Each set of (x, y) coordinates below is generated by a linear rule. For each set of coordinates, write an equation to describe the rule.

   a. $(-1, -7), (0, -3), (1, 1), (2, 5), (4, 13), (5, 17)$

   b. $(-2, 19), (-1, 14), (0, 9), (2, -1), (4, -11), (6, -21)$

   c. $(-2, -1), (0, 3), (1, 5), (3, 9), (5, 13), (6, 15)$

For Exercises 6–8, use the graph below.

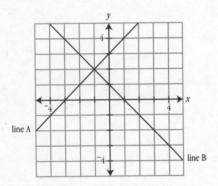

6. Make a table showing the coordinates of four points located on line A. What is the equation for line A?

Additional Practice (continued)

7. Make a table showing the coordinates of four points located on line B. What is the equation for line B?

8. Is there a point with (x, y) coordinates that satisfies both the equation for line A and the equation for line B? Explain your reasoning.

9. Martin used some rules to generate the following tables:

i.

x	y
⁻1	6
0	8
1	10
2	12
3	14

ii.

x	y
0	5
3	5
6	5
9	5
12	5

iii.

x	y
⁻2	⁻5
⁻1	⁻4.5
0	⁻4
3	⁻2.5
4	⁻2
5	⁻1.5

iv.

x	y
⁻1	0.5
0	0
1	0.5
2	2
3	4.5
4	8
5	12.5

a. Make a graph of the data in each table. Show the graphs on the same coordinate axes.

b. Which sets of data represent a linear relationship? How do you know?

Skill: Linear Relationships

Does the point represent a point on the graph of $y = x - 4$.

1. $(0, -4)$ **2.** $(5, -1)$ **3.** $(-3, -7)$ **4.** $(-7, -3)$

5. You order books through a catalog. Each book costs $12 and the shipping and handling cost is $5. Write an equation and make a graph that represents your total cost.

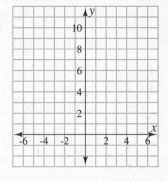

   a. What is the total cost if you buy 6 books?

   b. What is the total cost if you buy 4 books?

6. A ride in a taxicab costs $2.50 for the first mile and $1.50 for each additional mile, or part of a mile. Write an equation and make a graph that represents the total cost.

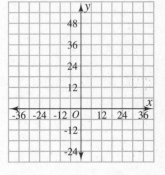

   a. What is the total cost of a 10-mile ride?

   b. What is the total cost of a 25-mile ride?

7. A tree is 3 feet tall and grows 3 inches each day. Write an equation and make a graph that represents how much the tree grows over time.

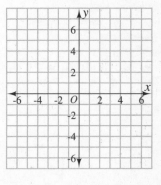

   a. How tall is the tree in a week?

   b. How tall is the tree in 4 weeks?

Write an equation for each graph.

8.

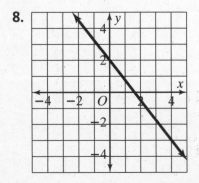

9.

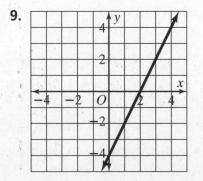

Additional Practice

1. Do parts (a)–(e) for each equation below.

   a. Graph the equation on your calculator, and make a sketch of the line you see.

   b. What ranges of *x*- and *y*-values did you use for your window?

   c. Do the *y*-values increase, decrease, or stay the same as the *x*-values increase?

   d. Give the *y*-intercept.

   e. List the coordinates of three points on the line.

   i. $y = 2.5x$

   ii. $y = -2x + 7$

   iii. $y = -4x - 8$

   iv. $y = 3x - 3$

Additional Practice (continued)

2. The volleyball team decided to raise money for an end-of-season party by selling school buttons. The costs and the revenue of selling the buttons are shown on the graph below.

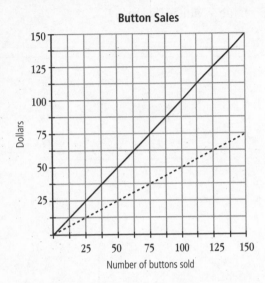

Button Sales

revenue

---- cost

a. If the team sells 50 buttons, what will be their cost? What will be the revenue?

b. If the team sells 50 buttons, how much profit will they make? (Remember that the profit is the revenue minus the cost).

c. If the team sells 100 buttons, how much profit will they make?

3. a. Graph the equation $y = 5x + 7$ on your calculator. Use the graph to find the missing coordinates for these points on the graph: $(2, ?)$, $(?, 52)$, and $(2.9, ?)$.

b. Graph the equation $y = 1.5x - 4$ on your calculator. Use the graph to find the missing coordinates for these points on the graph: $(10, ?)$ and $(?, 32)$.

c. Graph the equation $y = 6.25 - 3x$ on your calculator. Use the graph to find the missing coordinates for these points on the graph: $(5, ?)$ and $(-2.75, ?)$.

4. Use the graph below to answer parts (a)–(d).

a. List the coordinates of three points on the line.

b. Which equation below is the equation of the line?

i. $y = x + 4$ **ii.** $y = 0.5x + 2$

iii. $y = 0.5x - 5$ **iv.** $y = 4 - 0.5x$

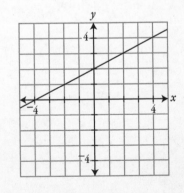

Additional Practice (continued)

c. Does the point $(56, 35)$ lie on the line? Explain.

d. Does the point $(-20, -8)$ lie on line? Explain.

5. Use the graph of the three lines to complete the table.

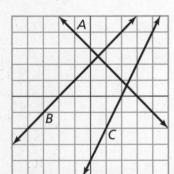

Line	Constant Rate of Change	y-intercept	x-intercept
A			
B			
C			

$$y = 2 + x, \quad y = -4 + 2x, \quad y = 3 - x$$

b. Match each line on the graph with one of the above equations.

line A: _____, line B: _____, line C: _____

6. Use the graph of the two lines at the right.

a. What is alike about these lines? What is different?

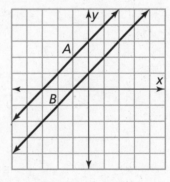

b. The equation for line A is $y = x + 3$. What do you think would have to change in the equation to make the equation for line B? Explain.

c. Write the equation for line B.

d. Imagine a line halfway between lines A and B. What is its equation? Explain.

Additional Practice *(continued)*

7. a. Use the graph below to complete the table.

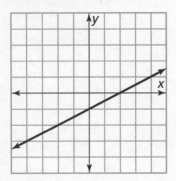

x	−3	0	2	5	7	10	100
y							

b. Explain your reasoning for the last three y-values.

8. a. For each pair of lines, find the point of intersection.

$y = x$ and $y = -x$

$y = x + 1$ and $y = -x + 1$

$y = x + 3$ and $y = -x + 3$

$y = x - 4$ and $y = -x - 4$

b. What pattern do you see?

c. Without graphing the lines, where is the point of intersection of these lines?

$y = x + 137$ and $y = -x + 137$

Skill: Linear Functions, Graphs, and Tables

1. A ride in a cab costs $0.40 plus $0.15 per mile.

   a. Write and graph an equation for traveling x miles in the cab.

   b. The cab charges $0.70 for a ride of how many miles?

   c. How much does the cab charge for a trip of 8 miles?

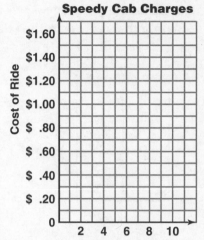

Speedy Cab Charges

Graph each linear equation.

2. $y = -4x + 6$

3. $y = -2x + 7$

4. $y = -3x - 1$

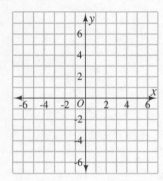
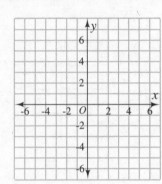
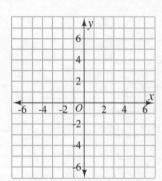

On which of the following lines does each point lie? A point may lie on more than one line.

   A. $y = x + 5$ **B.** $y = -x + 7$ **C.** $y = 2x - 1$

5. $(0, 5)$

6. $(1, 6)$

7. $\frac{8}{3}, \frac{13}{3}$

8. $(0, -1)$

9. $(4, 9)$

10. $(4, 3)$

11. $(-2, -5)$

12. $(-8, 15)$

Skill: Linear Functions, Graphs, and Tables (continued)

Decide if each table represents a linear relationship. For those that do, write an equation that represents the relationship.

13.

x	y
−3	18
−1	6
1	−6
3	−18

14.

x	y
5	−2
7	0
9	2
11	4

15.

x	y
−3	−17
−1	−11
1	−5
3	1

16.

x	y
−4	4
0	6
2	7
3	8

Additional Practice

1. The equations below represent the costs to print brochures at three different printers.

   a. For which equation does the point $(20, 60)$ lie on the graph? Explain.

   i. $C = 15 + 2.50N$ **ii.** $C = 50 + 1.75N$ **iii.** $C = 30 + 1.50N$

   b. For each equation, give the coordinates of a point on the graph of the equation.

2. The equations below represent the distances in meters traveled after t seconds by three cyclists.

   a. For which equation does the point $(10, 74)$ lie on the graph? Explain.

   i. $D = 2.4t + 32$ **ii.** $D = 4.2t + 32$ **iii.** $D = 6t + 32$

   b. For each equation, give the coordinates of a point on the graph of the equation.

3. Do parts (a) and (b) for each pair of equations below.

   i. $y = -\frac{12}{5}x - 6$ **ii.** $y = x - 3$

         $y = 4x + 14$ $y = -1.5x + 12$

   a. Graph the two equations on the same axes. Use window settings that allow you to see the points where the graphs intersect. What ranges of x- and y-values did you use for your window?

   b. Find the point of intersection of the graphs.

   iii. $y = x + 9$ **iv.** $y = 2x - 6$

         $y = 7 - 3x$ $y = -2$

   c. Test each point of intersection you found by substituting its coordinates into the equations. Did the points fit the equation exactly? Explain why or why not.

4. **a.** Find r if $2r + 10 = 22$.   **b.** Find x if $4.5x = 45$.

   c. Find z if $3z - 19 = 173$.   **d.** Find w if $67.1 = 29.7 - 0.2w$.

Additional Practice (continued)

5. Betty is thinking of two consecutive integers whose sum is 41. Let x represent the smaller unknown integer.

   a. How could you represent the larger unknown integer in terms of x?

   b. Write an equation showing that the sum of the two unknown integers is 41.

   c. Solve your equation. What integers is Betty thinking of?

6. Find the number described in each problem by writing and solving an equation.

   a. If Sarah subtracts five times her number from 24, she gets 4. What is Sarah's number?

   b. Twice Bill's number added to 17 is 7. What is Bill's number?

   c. The sum of 4 times a number and 14 is 16. What is the number?

   d. If Susan subtracts 11 from one fourth of her number she gets 11. What is Susan's number?

7. The school drama club is performing a play at the community theater. Props cost $250, and the theater is charging the drama club $1.25 for each ticket sold. So, the total cost C for the drama club to put on the play is $C = 1.25N + 250$, where N is the number of tickets sold. Customers pay $4 for each ticket, so the total amount collected from ticket sales is $T = 4N$.

   a. What is the cost if 213 tickets are sold?

   b. How much are the total ticket sales if 213 tickets are sold?

   c. What is the drama club's profit or loss if 213 tickets are sold?

   d. If the total ticket sales are $780, how many people attended the play?

   e. What is the cost of putting on the play for the number of people you found in part (d)?

Additional Practice (continued)

f. How many tickets does the drama club need to sell to break even?

g. The drama club would like to earn a profit of $500 from the play. How many tickets need to be sold for the club to meet this goal?

8. In each pair of equations, solve the first equation and graph the second equation:

a. $0 = 3x + 6$ $y = 3x + 6$

b. $0 = x - 2$ $y = x - 2$

c. $0 = 3x + 10$ $y = 3x + 10$

d. In each pair, how is the solution to the first equation related to the graph?

9. Marsha said there are two ways to solve the equation $3x + 15 = 24$.

$3x + 15 = 24$ Subtract 15 from each side. $3x + 15 = 24$ Divide each side by 3.

      $3x = 9$ Divide each side by 3. $x + 5 = 8$ Subtract 5 from each side.

       $x = 3$ $x = 3$

a. Are both strategies correct? Explain.

b. Which strategy do you think is easier? Explain.

c. How do you know when you can divide first?

d. Solve this equation in two ways: $5x + 20 = 5$

10. Find x if

   a. $x + 7 = 20$ **b.** $3x + 7 = 20$ **c.** $-2x + 7 = 20$

   d. How are the solutions similar? How are they different?

Additional Practice *(continued)*

11. If $y = \frac{2}{3}x + 4$, find y if

    a. $x = 0$ **b.** $x = 3$ **c.** $x = 9$

    d. $x = -9$ **e.** $x = 10$ **f.** $x = \frac{1}{2}$

12. Solve the following equations for the value of x:

    a. $3x + 5 = 4x - 10$

    b. $4x + 10 = 6x - 8$

    c. $3x + 10 = 5x$

    d. $3x - 11 = 8x - 21$

    e. $3(x + 8) = 12$

Skill: Exploring Equality

1. Determine whether each point is a solution of $y = 3x - 8$.

   a. $(0, -8)$ **b.** $(6, -10)$ **c.** $(-2, -2)$ **d.** $(4, 4)$

2. Determine whether each point is a solution of $y = -5x + 19$.

   a. $(-3, 4)$ **b.** $(0, 19)$ **c.** $(2, 9)$ **d.** $(-4, 39)$

Use the equation $y = -2x + 1$. Complete each solution.

3. $(0, \square)$ **4.** $(-5, \square)$ **5.** $(20, \square)$ **6.** $(-68, \square)$

Use each equation. Find y for $x = 1, 2, 3,$ and 4.

7. $y = 2x$ **8.** $y = 3x + 1$

9. $y = x - 5$ **10.** $y = -5x + 6$

Skill: Finding the Point of Intersection

Is each ordered pair a solution of the given system? Write *yes* or *no*.

1. $y = 6x + 12$

$2x - y = 4$

2. $y = -3x$

$x = 4y + \frac{1}{2}$

3. $x + 2y = 2$

$2x + 5y = 2$

$(-4, -12)$

$\left(-\frac{1}{2}, \frac{3}{2}\right)$

$(6, -2)$

4. Solve the system by graphing. Check your solution.

$x + y = 3$

$x - y = -1$

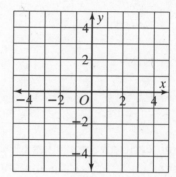

5. Tomatoes are $0.80 per pound at Rob's Market, and $1.20 per pound at Sal's Produce. You have a coupon for $1.40 off at Sal's. (Assume that you buy at least $1.40 worth of tomatoes.)

a. Write an equation relating the cost y to the number of pounds x at each market.

Rob's: Sal's:

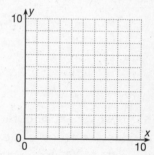

b. Use a graph to estimate the number of pounds for which the cost is the same at either store.

Skill: Solving Linear Equations

Solve each equation. Check your answers.

1. $10 + 5h = 25$

2. $8s - 8 = 64$

3. $3y + 78 = 81$

4. $2g + 4 = 12$

5. $5j + 5 = 15$

6. $3w + 8 = 20$

7. For a walk-a-thon a sponsor committed to give you a flat fee of \$5 plus \$2 for every mile you walk. Write an expression for the total amount of money you will collect from your sponsor at the end of the walk-a-thon. Then evaluate your expression for 20 miles walked.

8. To win the neighborhood tomato-growing contest Johnny needs for his tomato plants to produce 8 tomatoes per week. He needs 30 tomatoes to win the contest. He already has 6 tomatoes. Write and solve an equation to find the number of weeks he needs to produce 30 tomatoes.

Skill: Solving Linear Equations (continued)

For Exercises 9–14, solve each equation.

9. $4r + 6 = 14$

10. $9y - 11 = 7$

11. $-5b - 6 = -11$

12. $-9i - 17 = -26$

13. $14.9 = 8.6 + 0.9m$

14. $15w - 21 = -111$

15. Hugo received $100 for his birthday. He then saved $20 per week until he had a total of $460 to buy a printer. Use an equation to show how many weeks it took him to save the money.

16. A health club charges a $50 initial fee plus $2 for each visit. Moselle has spent a total of $144 at the health club this year. Use an equation to find how many visits she has made.

Additional Practice

1. Find the slope and y-intercept of the line represented by each equation.

   a. $y = 2x - 10$ **b.** $y = 4x + 3$ **c.** $y = 4x - 4.5$

   d. $y = 2.6x$ **e.** $y = 7x + 1$

2. Each table in (i.)–(v.) below represents a linear relationship. Do parts (a)–(c) for each table.

   a. Find the slope of the line that represents the relationship.

   b. Find the y-intercept for the graph of the relationship.

   c. Determine which of the following equations represents the relationship:

   $y = 3 - 4x$ $y = x + 6$ $y = 4x - 3$ $y = 3x - 1.5$ $y = 2.5x$

i.

x	y
0	0
1	2.5
2	5
3	7.5
4	10

ii.

x	y
0	6
1	7
2	8
3	9
4	10

iii.

x	y
0	⁻1.5
1	1.5
2	4.5
3	7.5
4	10.5

iv.

x	y
0	3
1	⁻1
2	⁻5
3	⁻9
4	⁻13

v.

x	y
1	1
2	5
3	9
4	13
5	17

Additional Practice (continued)

3. For each of the lines below, find the slope, and write an equation that represents the line.

a.

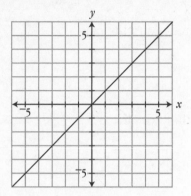

b.

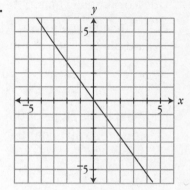

c.

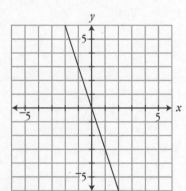

4. Do parts (a)–(d) for each pair of points below.

  a. Plot the points on a coordinate grid, and draw the line through the points.

  b. Find the slope of the line through the points.

  c. Estimate the *y*-intercept from the graph.

  d. Using your answers from parts (a) and (b), write an equation for the line through the points.

   i. $(0, 0)$ and $(-3, -3)$

   ii. $(1, -1)$ and $(-3, 3)$

Additional Practice (continued)

5. On Saturdays, Jim likes to go to the mall to play video games or pinball. Round-trip bus fare to and from the mall is $1.80. Jim spends $0.50 for each video or pinball game.

   a. Write an equation for the amount of money M it costs Jim to go to the mall and play n video or pinball games.

   b. What is the slope of the line your equation represents? What does the slope tell you about this situation?

   c. What is the y-intercept of the line? What does the y-intercept tell you about the situation?

   d. How much will it cost Jim to travel to the mall and play 8 video or pinball games?

   e. If Jim has $6.75, how many video or pinball games can he play at the mall?

6. At the right is a graph showing the total cost (including bus fare and the cost of comics) for Angie to go to the Comic Shop to buy new comic books.

   a. What is Angie's round-trip bus fare? Explain your reasoning.

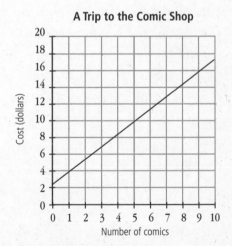

A Trip to the Comic Shop

   b. How much does a comic book cost at the Comic Shop? Explain.

   c. Write an equation that shows how much money M it costs Angie to buy n comic books at the Comic Shop. What information did you use from the graph to write the equation?

Additional Practice *(continued)*

7. Tonya is siphoning all the water from a full aquarium to clean it. The graph at the right shows the amount of water left in the aquarium as Tonya siphons the water.

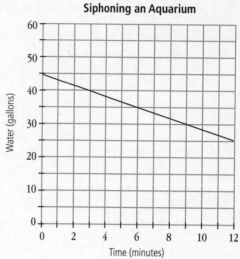

Siphoning an Aquarium

a. How much water was in the aquarium when it was full? Explain.

b. How much water does the siphon remove from the aquarium in 1 minute? Explain.

c. Write an equation that shows the amount of water G left in the aquarium after t minutes.

d. How many gallons of water are left in the aquarium after 10 minutes?

e. How long will it take the siphon to remove all of the water from the aquarium? Explain.

8. For parts (a)–(f), write an equation for the line that satisfies the given conditions.

a. The slope is 7 and the y-intercept is -2.

b. The slope is 0 and the y-intercept is 9.18.

c. The line passes through the points $(3, 1)$ and $(6, 4)$.

d. The line passes through the points $(-24, -11)$ and $(-8, -3)$.

e. The line passes through the points $(-4.5, 2)$ and $(6.3, 5.8)$.

f. The slope is $-\frac{2}{3}$ and the line passes through the point $(5, 0)$.

Additional Practice (continued)

9. Write an equation for each of the four lines shown on the graph below.

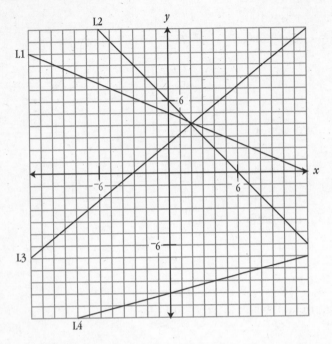

10. At Midtown Bowling Center, the cost to bowl four games is $8.40, and the cost to rent shoes is $1.15.

   a. Write an equation for the cost C for renting shoes and bowling n games.

   b. What is the y-intercept for your equation, and what does it represent?

   c. What is the slope of your equation, and what does the slope represent?

   d. What is the cost of renting shoes and bowling six games?

   e. Tony paid $7.45 for his games and shoe rental. How many games did Tony bowl?

Additional Practice (continued)

11. Here are some possible descriptions of a line:

   A. positive slope

   B. slope equals 0

   C. negative slope

   D. positive y-intercept

   E. y-intercept equals 0

   F. negative y-intercept

   G. passes through the origin: $(0, 0)$

   H. crosses the x-axis to the right of the origin

   K. crosses the x-axis to the left of the origin

   L. never crosses the x-axis

For each equation below, list ALL of the properties that describe the graph of that equation.

   a. $y = x$

   b. $y = 2x + 1$

   c. $y = -5$

   d. $y = 4 - 3x$

   e. $y = -3 - x$

12. a. These two points determine a line: $(0, 3)$ and $(2, 5)$. Which of these points is also on that line?

      $(4, 7)$ $(4, 8)$ $(4, 10)$

   b. These two points determine a line: $(-2, 10)$ and $(1, 4)$. Which of these points is also on that line?

      $(2, 0)$ $(2, 2)$ $(2, 10)$

Additional Practice (continued)

13. Below are four patterns:

Pattern 1:

Figure 1   Figure 2   Figure 3

Pattern 2:

Figure 1   Figure 2   Figure 3

Pattern 3:

Figure 1   Figure 2   Figure 3

Pattern 4:

Figure 1   Figure 2   Figure 3

a. In each cell in the chart below, write the PERIMETER of the figure:

Shape	Figure 1	Figure 2	Figure 3	Figure 4	Figure 10	Figure 100
Pattern 1						
Pattern 2						
Pattern 3						
Pattern 4						

b. Describe the pattern of change within each pattern.

c. Explain how you found the values for the last three columns.

d. Write an equation for the PERIMETER of figures for each pattern.

Additional Practice (continued)

14. Line A is the graph of this equation: $y = 2x + 2$.
Line B is the graph of this equation: $y = 2x$.

   a. What is alike about lines A and B? What is different?

   b. Write the equation of a line that lies between line A and line B. How is
your equation similar to the equations above? How is it different?

   c. Explain why your equation is correct.

Skill: Finding Slope

Find the slope of each line.

1.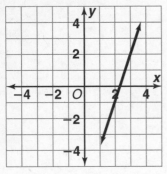

2.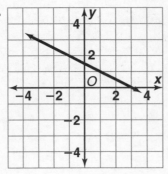

3.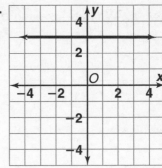

4.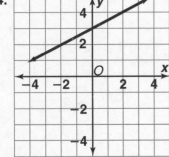

5.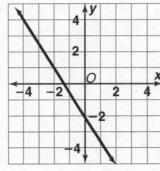

Skill: Finding Slope *(continued)*

For Exercises 6–7, the points from each table
lie on a line. Use the table to find the slope
of each line. Then graph the line.

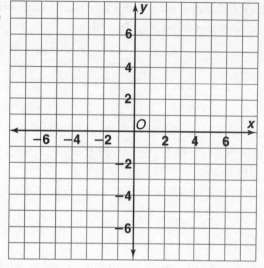

6.

x	0	1	2	3	4
y	−3	−1	1	3	5

slope =

7.

x	0	1	2	3	4
y	5	3	1	−1	−3

slope =

Find the slope of the line that passes through each pair of points.

8. $A(1, 1), B(6, 3)$

9. $J(−4, 6), K(−4, 2)$

10. $P(3, −7), Q(−1, −7)$

11. $M(7, 2), N(−1, 3)$

Skill: Using Slope

For Exercises 1–4, determine if the line that represents each equation has the same slope as the equation $y = 2x - 4$.

1. $y = 2x + 4$ **2.** $y = -2x + 3$ **3.** $y = 4x - 2$ **4.** $y = 3x - 4$

5. Which hill would it be easiest to push a heavy cart up, one with a slope of $\frac{1}{2}$, $\frac{1}{6}$, 3, or 5? Explain.

6. Which ski run would probably give you the greatest speed down a hill when you are skiing, one with a slope of $\frac{1}{8}$, $\frac{1}{4}$, 1, or 2?

7. Which roof would be the most dangerous for a roofer, one with a slope of $\frac{1}{16}$, $\frac{1}{10}$, $\frac{1}{2}$, or $\frac{3}{2}$?

8. Which of the slopes from Exercise 7 would be the easiest for the roofer?

Draw a line with the given slope through the given point.

9. $P(5, 1)$, slope $= -\frac{1}{3}$ **10.** $K(-2, 4)$, slope $= 3$

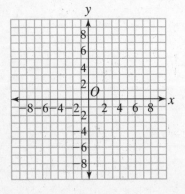 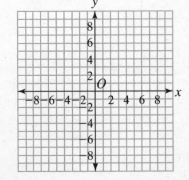

Skill: Writing Equations

Write an equation for each line.

1.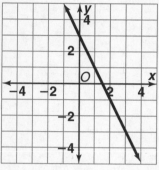

2.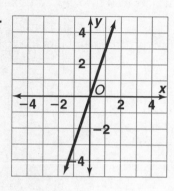

3.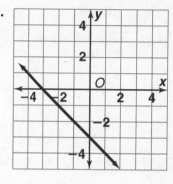

Use the graph at the right for Exercises 4–8.

4. What earnings will produce $225 in savings?

5. How much is saved from earnings of $400?

6. What is the slope of the line in the graph?

7. For each increase of $200 in earnings, what is the increase in savings?

8. Write an equation for the line.

Earned vs. Saved

Additional Practice

1. At the bottom of the page are four nets that will fold into rectangular boxes. Net *iii* folds into an open box. The other nets fold into closed boxes. Answer the following questions for each net.

   a. What are the dimensions of the box that can be made from the net?

   b. What is the surface area of the box?

   c. What total number of unit cubes would be needed to fill the box?

i.

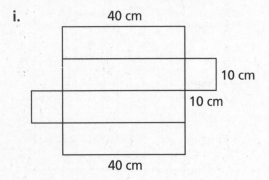

ii.

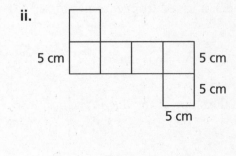

iii.

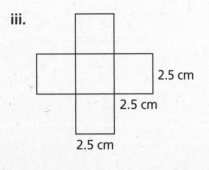

iv.

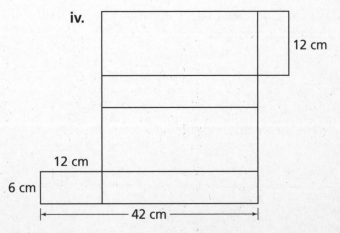

Additional Practice (continued)

2. a. Gina has a sheet of cardboard that measures 9 feet by 6 feet. She uses scissors and tape to make the entire sheet of cardboard into a closed box that is a perfect cube. What is the surface area of the box?

b. What is the length of each edge of the box? Explain your reasoning.

c. How many unit cubes would it take to fill the box?

3. a. Bill has a sheet of cardboard with an area of 10 square feet. He makes the entire sheet of cardboard into a closed rectangular box. The four sides of the box have the same area, and the two ends have the same area. The area of each of the four equal sides is twice the area of each end. What is the area of each face of Bill's box?

b. What are the dimensions of Bill's box?

c. How many unit cubes would it take to fill the box?

Skill: Area Review

Find the area of each figure.

1.
4 m
4 m

2.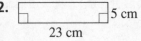
5 cm
23 cm

3.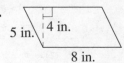
5 in. 4 in.
8 in.

4.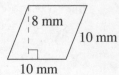
8 mm
10 mm
10 mm

5.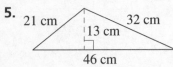
21 cm   32 cm
13 cm
46 cm

6.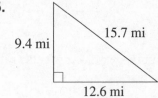
9.4 mi   15.7 mi
12.6 mi

7.
12.9 km   8.0 km
8.7 km
6.7 km
3.4 km

8.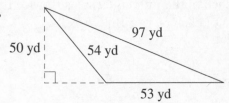
50 yd   97 yd
54 yd
53 yd

9.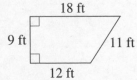
18 ft
9 ft   11 ft
12 ft

10.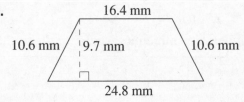
16.4 mm
10.6 mm   9.7 mm   10.6 mm
24.8 mm

Skill: Area Review *(continued)*

Find the area of each figure.

11.

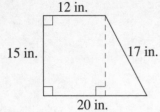

12.

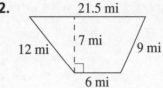

13.

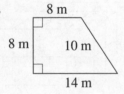

14.

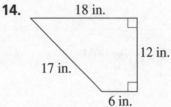

Find the perimeter and area of each figure.

15.

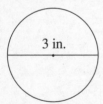

16.

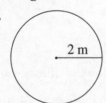

17.

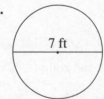

18.

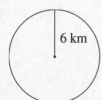

19.

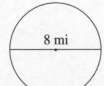

20.

Additional Practice

1. The bottom of a closed rectangular box has an area of 50 square centimeters. If the box is 8 centimeters high, give at least three possibilities for the dimensions of the box.

2. a. The rectangular prism at the right is made from centimeter cubes. What are the dimensions of the prism?

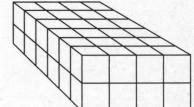

b. What is the surface area of the prism?

c. What is the volume of the prism? That is, how many cubes are in the prism?

d. Give the dimensions of a different rectangular prism that can be made from the same number of cubes. What is the surface area of the prism?

3. Use the diagram at the right to answer the following questions.

a. What is the total surface area of the box, including the bottom and the top?

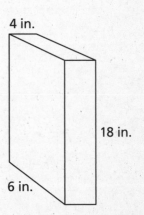

4 in.

18 in.

6 in.

b. How many inch cubes would it take to fill the box? Explain your reasoning.

Additional Practice (continued)

4. a. Each small cube in the rectangular prism at the right has edges of length 2 centimeters. What are the dimensions of the prism in centimeters?

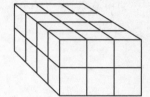

b. What is the surface area of the prism in square centimeters?

c. How many 1-centimeter cubes would it take to make a prism with the same dimensions as this prism? Explain your reasoning.

5. Answer parts (a) and (b) for each closed box below.

i.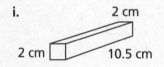

ii.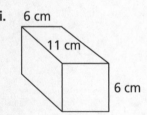

iii.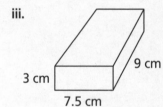

a. What is the surface area of each box?

b. What is the volume of each box

Additional Practice (continued)

6. For each number of cubes below, arrange the cubes in a rectangular prism so that a box which holds those cubes would require the least material to completely cover it. Sketch the arrangement and give the dimensions.

 a. 5   **b.** 6

 c. 7   **d.** 8

7. If you have N cubes, one arrangement that always forms a rectangular prism is $1 \times 1 \times N$. For what values of N is this the only such arrangement? Explain.

Skill: Surface Area of a Box

Draw a net for each prism.

1.

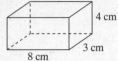

4 cm

3 cm

8 cm

2.

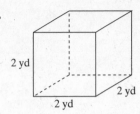

2 yd

2 yd

2 yd

Find the surface area of each figure to the nearest whole unit.

3.

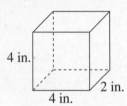

4 in.

4 in.

2 in.

4.

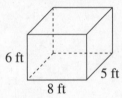

6 ft

8 ft

5 ft

5.

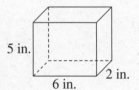

5 in.

6 in.

2 in.

6.

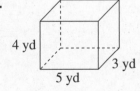

4 yd

5 yd

3 yd

Skill: Surface Area of a Box (continued)

Find the surface area of each prism.

7.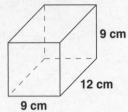

9 cm
12 cm
9 cm

8.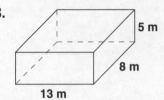

5 m
8 m
13 m

9.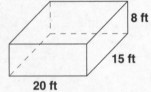

8 ft
15 ft
20 ft

10.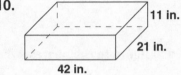

11 in.
21 in.
42 in.

11.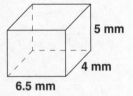

5 mm
4 mm
6.5 mm

12.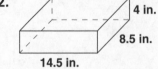

4 in.
8.5 in.
14.5 in.

Skill: Volume of a Box

Find the volume of each closed box.

1.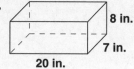

8 in.

7 in.

20 in.

2.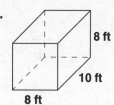

8 ft

10 ft

8 ft

3.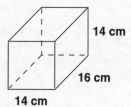

14 cm

16 cm

14 cm

4.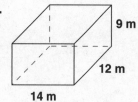

9 m

12 m

14 m

Skill: Volume of a Box

Skill: Volume of a Box (continued)

Find the volume of each closed box.

5.

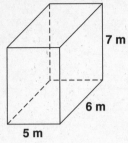

7 m

6 m

5 m

6.

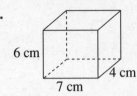

6 cm

7 cm

4 cm

7.

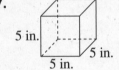

5 in.

5 in.

5 in.

8.

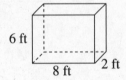

6 ft

8 ft

2 ft

Additional Practice

1. What is the volume of the prism below? Explain your reasoning.

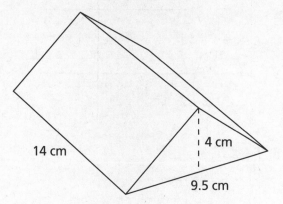

14 cm

4 cm

9.5 cm

2. The volume of a prism is 275 cubic centimeters. The area of the base of the prism is 25 square centimeters. What is the height of the prism? Explain.

3. Give the dimensions of three different rectangular prisms that have a volume of 240 cubic centimeters.

4. a. The circumference of the base of a cylinder is 16 centimeters. The height of the cylinder is 10 centimeters. What is the surface area of the cylinder?

   b. What is the volume of the cylinder?

Additional Practice (continued)

5. Use the closed cylinders below to answer parts (a) and (b).

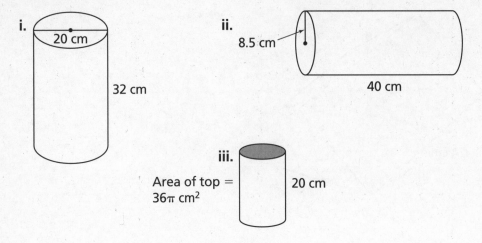

i. 20 cm 32 cm

ii. 8.5 cm 40 cm

iii. Area of top = 36π cm² 20 cm

   a. What is the surface area of each cylinder?

   b. What is the volume of each cylinder?

6. a. A cylindrical storage tank has a radius of 1 meter and a height of 3 meters. What is the surface area of the storage tank?

   b. What is the volume of the storage tank?

7. a. A cylinder without a top has a height of 25 centimeters and a circumference of 10π centimeters. What is the surface area of the cylinder?

   b. What is the volume of the cylinder?

Additional Practice *(continued)*

8. Below are three triangular prisms (not drawn to scale). The height of the first prism is 8 units, and the volumes of all three prisms are the same. What are the heights of the other two prisms?

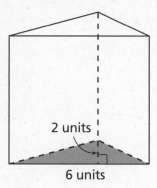
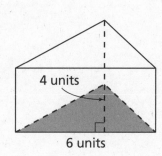
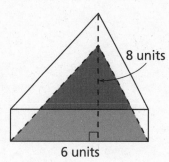

9. Below are three triangular prisms (not drawn to scale). The height of the first prism is 8, and the volumes of all three prisms are the same. What are the heights of the other two prisms?

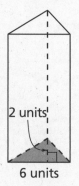
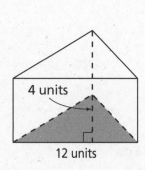
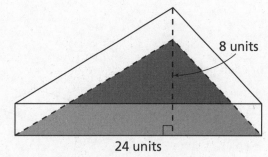

Skill: Volume of a Prism or a Cylinder

Name each three-dimensional figure.

1.

2.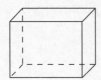

3.

4.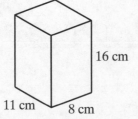

Find the volume of each prism or cylinder.

5.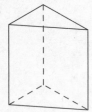

10 m

8 m

6.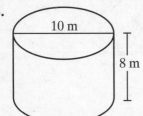

16 cm

11 cm   8 cm

Skill: Volume of a Prism or a Cylinder (continued)

For Exercises 7–10, find the volume of each prism or cylinder.

7.

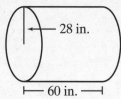

28 in.

⊢— 60 in. —⊣

8.

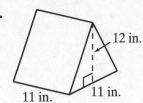

12 in.

11 in.   11 in.

9.

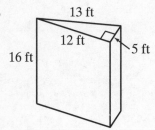

13 ft

12 ft

16 ft

5 ft

10.

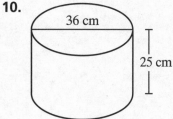

36 cm

25 cm

11. A water storage tank has a cylindrical shape. The base has a diameter of 18 meters and the tank is 32 meters high. How much water, to the nearest cubic unit, can the tank hold?

12. A cylindrical juice container is 9 inches tall and has a radius of 2 inches. What is the volume of the container to the nearest whole unit?

Skill: Nets and Surface Area

Name the three-dimensional shape you can form from each net.

1.

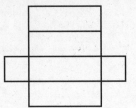

2.

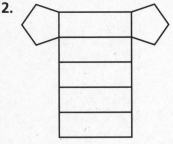

3.

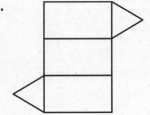

4.

5.

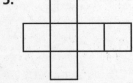

Skill: Nets and Surface Area (continued)

Find the surface area of each figure to the nearest square unit.

6.

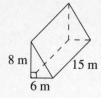

8 m   15 m   6 m

7.

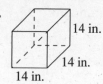

14 in.   14 in.   14 in.

8.

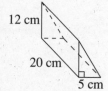

12 cm   20 cm   5 cm

9.

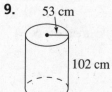

53 cm   102 cm

10.

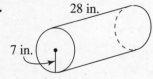

28 in.   7 in.

11.

d = 44 ft   50 ft

Additional Practice

1. Find the volume of each of the following:

   a. a sphere with a radius of 4 centimeters

   b. a cone with a height of 10 inches and a base of radius 3 inches

   c. a cylinder with a base area of 10π square centimeters and a height of 25 centimeters

   d. a sphere with a diameter of 100 centimeters

   e. a cylinder with a radius of 14 inches and a height of 1.5 feet

   f. a cone with a base area of 11.5π square centimeters and a height of 20 centimeters

2. Find the volume of each of the following figures.

   a.

   3 cm

   b.

   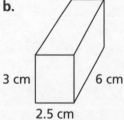

   3 cm   6 cm

   2.5 cm

Additional Practice (continued)

c.

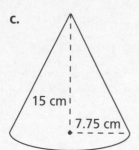

15 cm

7.75 cm

d.

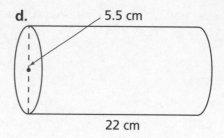

5.5 cm

22 cm

3. a. A tepee is a conical shaped tent used for shelter by the Plains Indians of North America. Suppose a tepee has a radius of 9 ft and is 10 ft high. How much floor space does the tepee have?

b. What is the volume of the tepee?

4. a. Assuming the two cones at the right are similar, what is the height of the smaller cone?

b. What is the volume of the larger cone?

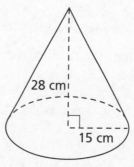

28 cm

15 cm

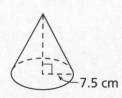

7.5 cm

c. What is the volume of the smaller cone?

d. Angie is using the smaller cone to scoop popcorn into the larger cone. How many scoops from the smaller cone will it take to fill the larger cone?

Additional Practice (continued)

5. A sphere has a diameter of 4 m. What is its volume?

6. a. Find the volume of this cylinder:

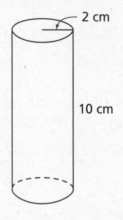

2 cm

10 cm

b. What is the volume if the height is doubled?

c. What is the volume if the radius of the base is doubled?

d. What is the volume if both the height and the radius of the base are doubled?

Skill: Cones, Pyramids, and Spheres

Find the volume of each figure to the nearest cubic unit.

1.

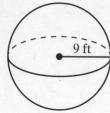

9 ft

2.

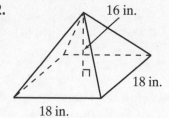

16 in.

18 in.

18 in.

3.

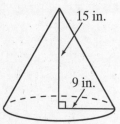

15 in.

9 in.

4.

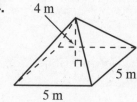

4 m

5 m

5 m

5.

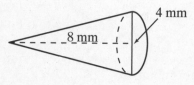

4 mm

8 mm

6.

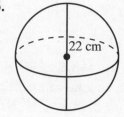

22 cm

Additional Practice

1. A closed rectangular box has a height of 2 feet, a length of 4 feet, and a width of 4 feet.

   a. What is the volume of the box? What is the surface area of the box?

   b. Give the dimensions of a closed rectangular box that has one-fourth the volume of this 2-4-4 box, and give the surface area of this smaller box.

   c. What is the ratio of the surface area of the 2-4-4 box to the surface area of the box you found in part (b)?

2. Lee built a box with a volume equal to 8 times the volume of a 2-1-5 box.

   a. What might be the dimensions of Lee's box?

   b. Is your answer to part (a) the only possibility for the dimensions of the larger box? Explain your reasoning.

3. A cone has a height of 12 centimeters and a base with a radius of 4 centimeters.

   a. The cone is scaled down to a similar cone with one-eighth of the original volume. What are the dimensions of the scaled-down cone?

   b. Is your answer to part (a) the only possibility for the dimensions of the scaled-down cone? Explain your reasoning.

4. **a.** How does the volume of a sphere with a radius of 4 centimeters compare to the volume of a sphere with a radius of 6 centimeters? Explain your reasoning.

   b. Are the 4-centimeter sphere and the 6-centimeter sphere similar? Explain your reasoning.

Additional Practice (continued)

5. When a ball is immersed in water, it displaces 36π cubic centimeters of water. What is the radius of the ball?

6. A conical cup is partially filled with water as shown in the diagram below. Use the diagram to answer the following questions.

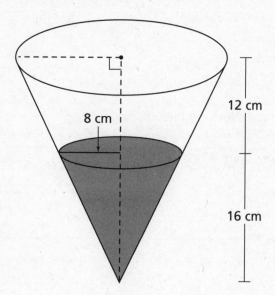

a. What is the radius of the top of the cup? Explain your reasoning.

b. What is the volume of the water in the cup?

c. What is the volume of the cup? Explain.

7. When a cube is dropped into a graduated cylinder partially filled with water, 125 ml of water are displaced. What is the length of each edge of the cube? Explain your reasoning.

8. a. Complete the table below for each rectangular box.

Closed Box	Surface Area	Volume
A: 1-2-3 box		
B: 2-4-6 box		
C: 3-6-9 box		
D: 4-8-12 box		

b. Use your table from part (a) to complete the table below.

Boxes to Compare	Ratio of Dimensions	Ratio of Surface Areas	Ratio of Volumes
B and A			
C and A			
D and A			
D and B			
C and B			
D and C			

c. What patterns do you see in the ratios?

Additional Practice

1. Josh is playing golf. He has 3 white golf balls, 4 yellow golf balls, and 1 red golf ball in his golf bag. At the first hole, he randomly draws a ball from his bag.

   a. What is the probability that he draws a white golf ball?

   b. What is the probability that he draws a red golf ball?

   c. What is the probability that he draws a yellow golf ball?

   d. On the sixth hole, Josh drives one of his white golf balls into a pond and has to draw another ball from his bag.

   i. What is the probability that he draws a white golf ball?

   ii. What is the probability that he draws a red golf ball?

   iii. What is the probability that he draws a yellow golf ball?

   e. Are the probabilities you found in parts (a)–(d) experimental probabilities or theoretical probabilities? Explain.

2. To help his 3-year-old sister Emily learn her colors, Kyle has put some yellow, green, red, and blue blocks in a bucket. Emily draws a block from the bucket, names its color, and puts the block back in the bucket. Then Kyle mixes the blocks, and Emily draws again. In playing this game 20 times, Emily draws a yellow block 6 times, a green block 2 times, a red block 8 times, and a blue block 4 times.

   a. Based on Emily's draws, what is the probability of drawing a yellow block from the bucket?

   b. What is the probability of drawing a green block from the bucket?

   c. What is the probability of drawing a red block from the bucket?

   d. What is the probability of drawing a blue block from the bucket?

   e. Are the probabilities you found in parts (a)–(d) experimental probabilities or theoretical probabilities? Explain.

Additional Practice *(continued)*

f. There are a total of 10 blocks in the bucket. Based on the results of Emily's 20 draws, how many yellow, green, red, and blue blocks would you expect to be in the bucket? Explain.

3. A pyramid has four faces that are congruent equilateral triangles. The faces of a game piece that is a pyramid are labeled with the numbers 1, 2, 3, and 4. A roll of the game piece is determined by the number on the face the game piece lands on. Below are the rules of a game played with two such game pieces.

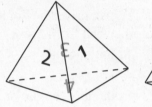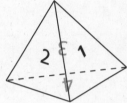

- Player I and Player II take turns rolling two 4-sided number cubes.
- If the sum of the numbers rolled is odd, Player I gets a point.
- If the sum of the numbers rolled is even, Player II gets a point.
- The player with the most points after 32 rolls wins.

a. Make a table that shows all the possible outcomes of rolling two 4-sided number cubes.

b. What is the probability of rolling a sum of 5?

c. What is the probability of rolling a sum of 4?

d. What is the probability of rolling a sum of 7?

e. Do you think the game is fair? Explain.

f. Suppose that, in 32 rolls, a sum of 8 is rolled twice. Is this unusual? Explain.

Additional Practice (continued)

4. a. Juanita is holding five coins with a total value of 27 cents. What is the probability that three of the coins are pennies? Explain.

b. What is the probability that one of the coins is a quarter? Explain.

5. Michelle flips a penny four times, and it lands heads up all four times. On her fifth flip, what is the probability that the penny will land tails up? Explain.

6. A standard deck of playing cards has 52 cards. The deck is divided into 4 suits: spades, hearts, diamonds, and clubs. There are 13 cards of each suit.

a. If you randomly draw a card from a standard deck of playing cards, what is the probability that you will draw a heart?

b. If you draw 12 cards, how many clubs could you expect to draw? Explain.

c. If you remove all the diamonds from a deck of cards and then draw 12 cards, how many clubs could you expect to draw? Explain.

d. Are the probabilities you found in parts (a)–(c) experimental probabilities or theoretical probabilities? Explain.

7. a. Sam started his own pizza shop. He has one kind of crust, one kind of sauce and six toppings: ground beef, pepperoni, onion, green peppers, mushrooms and fresh basil. How many different two-topping pizzas can he make?

b. Sam soon decides to offer three kinds of sauce: regular, spicy and extra spicy. How many kinds of two-topping pizzas can he make with sauce?

c. Finally, Sam decides to offer two kinds of crust: regular and whole-wheat. Now how many kinds of two-topping pizzas can he make?

Skill: Experimental and Theoretical Probability

Mirga and José played a game and made this table.

1. Find the experimental probability that Mirga wins.

Mirga wins	ℍℍ ℍℍ ℍℍ ℍℍ ℍℍ I
José wins	ℍℍ I
Times played	ℍℍ ℍℍ ℍℍ ℍℍ ℍℍ ℍℍ II

2. Find the experimental probability that José wins.

3. Do you think the game is fair? Explain.

The table below shows the results of spinning a spinner 15 times. Find each experimental probability.

Trial	1	2	3	4	5	6	7	8
Outcome	blue	yellow	red	blue	green	red	yellow	blue

Trial	9	10	11	12	13	14	15
Outcome	blue	green	red	blue	blue	green	red

4. $P(\text{red})$　　　　　**5.** $P(\text{yellow})$　　　　　**6.** $P(\text{green})$

Skill: Experimental and Theoretical Probability *(cont.)*

You spin a spinner with 10 sections numbered 1 through 10. Each outcome
(section) is equally likely. Find the probabilities below as a fraction, decimal,
and percent.

7. $P(9)$

8. $P(\text{even})$

9. $P(\text{number greater than 0})$

10. $P(\text{multiple of 4})$

There are eight blue marbles, nine orange marbles, and six yellow marbles in a
bag. You draw one marble. Find each probability.

11. $P(\text{blue marble})$

12. $P(\text{yellow marble})$

13. What marble could you add or remove so that the probability of drawing a
blue marble is $\frac{1}{3}$?

Skill: Counting Outcomes

Draw a tree diagram to show all possibilities.

1. Today, the school's cafeteria is offering a choice of pizza or spaghetti. You can get milk or juice to drink. For dessert you can get pudding or an apple. You must take one of each choice.

2. A clothing store sells shirts in three sizes: small, medium, and large. The shirts come with buttons or with snaps. The colors available are blue or beige.

A computer store sells 4 models of a computer (m1, m2, m3, and m4). Each model can be fitted with 3 sizes of hard drive (A, B, and C).

3. Draw a tree diagram.

4. What is the probability of choosing a computer with a size C hard drive at random?

5. What is the probability of choosing a model 2 computer with a size A hard drive at random?

Additional Practice

1. Shawon has a spinner that is divided into four regions. He spins the spinner several times and records his results in a table.

Region	Number of Times Spinner Lands in Region
1	9
2	4
3	12
4	11

a. Based on Shawon's results, what is the probability of the spinner landing on region 1?

b. What is the probability of the spinner landing on region 2?

c. What is the probability of the spinner landing on region 3?

d. What is the probability of the spinner landing on region 4?

e. Are the probabilities you found in parts (a)–(d) theoretical probabilities or experimental probabilities?

f. Make a drawing of what Shawon's spinner might look like.

Additional Practice *(continued)*

2. Irene randomly tosses a cube onto the grid below.

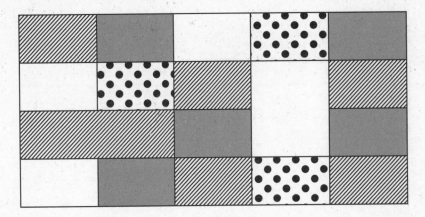

a. What is the probability of the cube landing on a striped rectangle? Express your answer as a percent.

b. What is the probability of the cube landing on a white rectangle? Express your answer as a percent.

c. What is the probability of the cube landing on a gray rectangle? Express your answer as a percent.

d. What is the probability of the cube landing on a dotted rectangle? Express your answer as a percent.

e. What is the probability of the cube not landing on a white rectangle? Express your answer as a percent.

f. What is the probability of the cube not landing on a striped rectangle? Express your answer as a percent.

g. Irene proposed the following game: If the cube lands on a striped square or a dotted square, Irene wins; if the cube lands on a white square or a gray square, Irene's sister wins. Is this a fair game? Explain your reasoning.

Additional Practice (continued)

3. Zark randomly selects one of the segments in the diagram leading from point
A. He follows that segment until he reaches another lettered point. Then, he
randomly selects one of the segments leading from that point and follows it to
the next lettered point. He continues this process until he reaches a dead end.
In parts (a)–(e) below, we use a series of letters to represent a path. For example,
the path *AEHI* is the path from *A* to *E* to *H* to *I*.

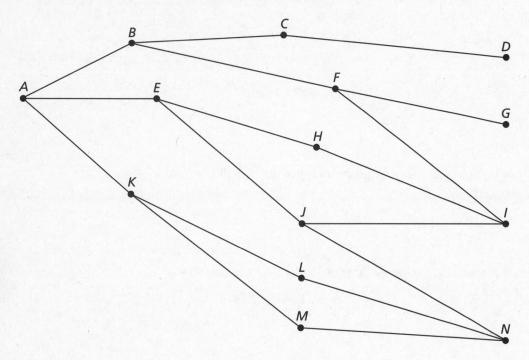

a. What is the probability that Zark followed path *AEJN*?

b. What is the probability that he followed path *ABCD*?

c. What is the probability that he followed path *ABFI*?

d. Are paths *AKLN* and *AKMN* equally likely to be selected? Explain your
reasoning.

e. If Zark repeats this process 50 times, how many times would you expect
him to follow path *AEJI*? Explain.

Additional Practice (continued)

4. a. If a letter is randomly selected from the letters A, B, C, D, and E, what is the probability that the letter will be B? Explain.

b. If a letter is selected by spinning the spinner at the right, what is the probability that the letter will be B? Explain.

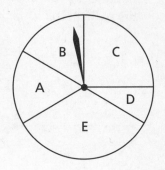

c. Are your answers to parts (a) and (b) the same? Explain.

d. If the spinner is spun once, what is the probability that it will not land in region C? Explain.

e. If the spinner is spun once, what is the probability that it will land in region D? Explain.

f. If the spinner is spun 100 times, how many times would you expect it to land in region E? Explain.

5. The faces of one six-sided number cube are labeled 1, 1, 1, 2, 2, 3, and the faces of a second cube are labeled 0, 1, 2, 2, 2, 3. The two cubes are rolled, and the results are added.

a. What is the probability of rolling a sum of 1?

b. What is the probability of rolling a sum of 6?

c. What is the probability of rolling a sum of 4?

d. What is the probability of rolling a sum that is not 1 or 6? Explain.

Skill: Area Models and Probability

What Do You Expect?

A spinner is divided into 5 equal sections. You spin the spinner once.

1. Find the probability that the spinner lands on a white section.

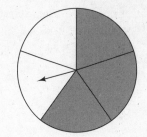

2. Find the probability that the spinner lands on a dark section.

A dart is thrown at the game board shown. Notice that the diameters are at right angles and the slices that are congruent. Find each probability.

3. *P(A)*

4. *P(B)*

5. *P(C)*

6. *P*(not *A*)

7. *P*(not *B*)

8. *P*(not *C*)

Additional Practice

1. a. Jennifer is on her school's softball team. So far this season, Jennifer has 38 hits in 75 times at bat. Based on her current batting average, what are Jennifer's chances of getting a hit next time she is at bat? Explain your reasoning.

   b. If Jennifer bats 5 times during a game, how many hits would you expect her to get? Explain.

   c. Next season, Jennifer wants to average 6 hits for every 10 times at bat. If she bats 80 times during the season, how many hits will she need to get to achieve her goal?

2. Aaron bowls on his school's bowling team. Based on statistics from past games, the probability that Aaron will knock down all ten pins on his first ball (a strike) is $\frac{2}{5}$. If he does not get a strike, the probability that he will knock down the remaining pins with his second ball (a spare) is $\frac{3}{4}$.

   a. In bowling, a turkey is three strikes in a row. If Aaron bowls three turns, what is the probability that he will get a turkey?

   b. Aaron had 8 chances to make spares during one of his league games. How many of the spares would you expect him to have made? Explain.

   c. In bowling, an open occurs when the bowler does not get a strike on the first ball and then does not get a spare on the second ball. When Aaron rolls two balls, what are his chances of getting an open?

   d. Suppose Aaron bowls 30 practice frames. When he does not get a strike, he tries to get a spare.

      i. How many strikes would you expect Aaron to get?

      ii. How many spares would you expect Aaron to get?

      iii. How many opens would you expect Aaron to get?

Additional Practice (continued)

3. In a game, two players take turns rolling two number cubes, each numbered 1 to 6. The numbers are added, and the sum is multiplied by 6. If the final result is an odd number, Player I gets 1 point. If the final result is an even number, Player II gets 1 point.

   a. List all the possible outcomes of a turn (that is, list the final results when the sum of two number cubes is multiplied by 6).

   b. What is the probability that the final number will be odd? What is the probability that the final number will be even? Explain.

   c. Is this a fair game?

4. The Alphabet Game costs $0.25 to play. Before the game, 26 slips of paper, each with a different letter of the alphabet on it, are put into a bag. A player draws one slip from the bag. If the player draws a vowel (A, E, I, O, or U), he or she wins $1.

   a. What is the probability of winning the game?

   b. What is the probability of losing the game?

   c. If a player plays the Alphabet Game 26 times, how much money would you expect the player to win or lose? Explain.

5. Suppose you play a game in which you toss 1 coin. You win $10 if it lands HEADS and you win nothing if it lands TAILS.

   a. If it costs $5 to play the game, would you expect to win or lose money in the long run? Explain.

   b. If it costs $10 to play the game, would you expect people to want to play the game? Explain.

   c. If it costs $6 to play the game, would you expect people to want to play the game? Explain.

   d. If it costs $4 to play the game, would you expect people to want to play the game? Explain.

Additional Practice (continued)

6. Suppose you play a game in which you toss 2 coins. You win $10 if the coins match, and you win nothing if the coins do not match.

   a. If it costs $5 to play the game, would you expect to win or lose money in the long run? Explain.

   b. If it costs $10 to play, would you expect people to want to play? Explain.

   c. If it costs $6 to play, would you expect people to want to play?

   d. If it costs $4 to play, would you expect people to want to play?

7. Suppose you play a game in which you toss 3 coins. You win $10 if the coins match (all HEADS or all TAILS), and you win nothing if the coins do not match.

   a. If it costs $5 to play the game, would you expect to win or lose money in the long run? Explain.

   b. If it costs $10 to play the game, would you expect people to want to play? Explain.

   c. How much should you charge to play the game, if you want players to "break even" in the long run?

8. Suppose you play a game in which you roll 1 number cube. You win $10 if the number on top is divisible by 3 without a remainder, and you win nothing otherwise.

   a. If it costs $5 to play the game, would you expect to win or lose money in the long run? Explain.

   b. If it costs $10 to play the game, would you expect people to want to play? Explain.

   c. If it costs $4 to play, would you expect people to want to play?

   d. If it costs $3 to play, would you expect people to want to play?

Additional Practice

1. Kathy runs cross country and plays basketball and softball. For each sport, she received a uniform with a randomly assigned number between 0 and 99 printed on it.

   a. What is the probability that all of Kathy's uniforms have odd numbers? Explain your reasoning.

   b. What is the probability that all of Kathy's uniforms have even numbers?

   c. What is the probability that one of Kathy's uniforms has an even number and the other two have odd numbers? Explain.

2. To play the Nickel Game, a player tosses two nickels at the same time. If both nickels land tails up, the player wins $1. If both nickels land heads up, the player wins $2. Otherwise, the player wins nothing.

   a. If it costs $1 to play the Nickel Game, how much could a player expect to win or lose if he or she plays the game 12 times? Explain.

   b. At next year's carnival, the game committee wants to charge prices that will allow players to break even. How much should they charge to play the Nickel Game? Explain.

3. In the Ring Toss game, a player tosses a ring at a group of bottles. If the ring goes over a bottle, the player wins a prize. The attendant at the Ring Toss game tells Ben that his chances of winning are 50% because when Ben tosses a ring, it will either go over a bottle or it will not. Do you believe the attendant? Explain.

Additional Practice (continued)

4. Two teams, Eagles and Falcons, are going to play a championship series of 3 games. The teams are evenly matched, so they have the same chance of winning each game.

   a. What is the probability that the Eagles win the first game? The Falcons?

   b. If the Eagles win the first game, what is the probability that the Eagles win the second game? The Falcons?

   c. If the Eagles win the first game, what is the probability that the series ends in two games?

   d. If the Eagles win the first game and the Falcons win the second game, what is the probability that the Eagles win the series?

   e. If the Eagles win the first game and the Falcons win the second game, what is the probability that the Falcons win the series?

5. Suppose the Eagles are twice as likely as the Falcons to win each game.

   a. What is the probability that the Eagles win the first game? The Falcons?

   b. If the Eagles win the first game, what is the probability that the Eagles win the second game? The Falcons?

   c. If the Eagles win the first game, what is the probability that the series ends in two games?

   d. If the Eagles win the first game and the Falcons win the second game, what is the probability that the Eagles win the series?

   e. If the Eagles win the first game and the Falcons win the second game, what is the probability that the Falcons win the series?

Additional Practice (continued)

6. a. Suppose the Crawfords have three children. Assume that the probability of a boy or a girl is $\frac{1}{2}$ for each birth. List the possible outcomes.

b. What is the probability that exactly two of the Crawfords' children are boys and the boys are born in a row?

c. What is the probability that the Crawfords have at least two boys born in a row?

d. Explain why the answers to parts (b) and (c) are not the same.

7. a. Suppose the Crawfords have four children. Assume that the probability of a boy or a girl is $\frac{1}{2}$ for each birth. List the possible outcomes.

b. What is the probability that exactly two of the Crawfords' children are boys and the boys are born in a row?

c. What is the probability that the Crawfords have at least two boys born in a row?

d. Explain why the answers to parts (b) and (c) are not the same.

Additional Practice

For Exercises 1 and 2, use the table below.

New M&M's® Candies

Bag #	Green	Yellow	Orange	Blue	Brown	Red	Total
1	14	7	8	10	17	3	59
2	14	10	16	7	7	3	57
3	14	17	7	11	9	2	60
4	13	13	8	11	6	7	58
5	15	11	7	15	6	5	59
6	11	6	16	14	5	5	57
7	20	9	8	13	7	2	59
8	10	14	8	14	10	3	59
9	17	11	8	14	10	3	63
10	17	10	14	14	4	2	61
11	14	11	11	5	9	7	57
12	9	7	20	8	12	1	57
13	12	13	9	17	7	2	60
14	8	8	12	11	17	4	60
15	18	8	13	9	7	4	59
TOTAL							

1. a. On a separate piece of paper, make a bar graph for each set of data for Bags 1, 2, and 3. Each bar graph shows the percent of all candies for each color found in that bag.

   b. Write two or more comparison statements that describe the data for the three bags of candy.

2. a. Determine the totals for each color of M&M's candies found in all 15 bags. On a separate piece of paper, make a bar graph for these data that shows percent of all candies for each color found in the fifteen bags.

   b. Describe the data by writing two or more comparison statements.

   c. Compare this graph with the graphs you made for the Bags 1, 2, and 3 of M&M's candies. Is there some plan to the distribution of colors in bags of M&M's candies? Explain your reasoning.

Additional Practice (continued)

For Exercises 3–5, use the table of data.

Immigrants to the United States

Decade	Immigrants From Canada	Total Immigrants	Percent of Immigrants From Canada
1820	209	8,385	2%
1821–30	2,277	143,439	2%
1831–40	13,624	599,125	2%
1841–50	41,723	1,713,251	2%
1851–60	59,309	2,598,214	2%
1861–70	153,878	2,314,824	7%
1871–80	383,640	2,812,191	14%
1881–90	393,304	5,246,613	7%
1891–1900	3,311	3,687,564	0%
1901–10	179,226	8,795,386	2%
1911–20	742,185	5,735,811	13%
1921–30	924,515	4,107,209	23%
1931–40	108,527	528,431	21%
1941–50	171,718	1,035,039	17%
1951–60	377,952	2,515,479	15%
1961–70	413,310	3,321,677	12%
1971–80	169,939	4,493,314	4%
1981–90	156,938	7,338,062	2%
1991–1996	127,481	9,095,417	1%

Source: Brownstone, D. M. & Franck, I. M. (2001). *Facts about the American immigration,* Bronx, NY: H. W. Wilson, p. 487.

3. a. In each of the decades from 1911–1920 and 1941–1950, how many people immigrated from Canada?

b. Add these bars to the bar graph of Exercise 5 titled, "Number of Immigrants from Canada."

Additional Practice (continued)

  c. Which of the statements below are true?

     i. There are more immigrants who came to the U.S. in the decade between 1911–20 than in 1941–50.

    ii. About the same number of immigrants came to the U.S. in the decade between 1911–20 and in the decade between 1941–50.

   iii. The number of immigrants in the decade between 1911-20 is about 250,000 more than the number of immigrants who came to the U.S. in the decade between 1941-50.

   iv. None of the above is true.

    v. All of the above are true.

4. a. In each of the decades from 1911-1920 and 1941-1950, how many people were immigrants to the U.S. from all countries?

  b. What percent of each of these numbers were immigrants from Canada?

  c. Add these bars to a copy of the bar graph from Exercise 5 titled, "Percentage of Immigrants from Canada in Total U.S. Immigration."

  d. Write two comparison statements about how these data values are similar to or different from the data values for other decades.

Additional Practice (continued)

5. a. How has the pattern of immigration from Canada to the United States changed between 1820 and 1996? Explain.

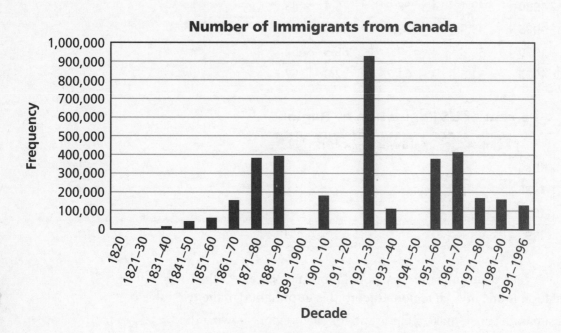

Number of Immigrants from Canada

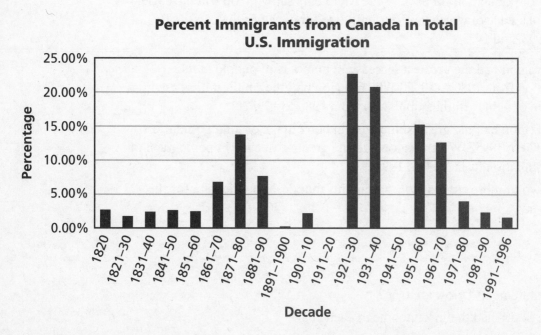

Percent Immigrants from Canada in Total U.S. Immigration

b. What does it mean that the bar for 1931–40 looks so different on the two bar graphs above?

Additional Practice (continued)

For Exercise 6, use the table.

US Population by Region (in millions)

	Northeast	Midwest	South	West	TOTAL
1980	49.1	58.9	75.4	43.2	
1985	49.9	58.8	81.4	47.8	
1990	50.8	59.7	85.5	52.8	
1995	51.5	61.7	92.0	57.7	

Percent of US Population by Region

	Northeast	Midwest	South	West
1980				
1985				
1990				
1995				

6. a. For each year, determine the total population and percent of the total population found in each region. Record this information in the two tables.

b. On a separate paper, make a bar graph for each region showing the percent of population for each of the four years shown. You will have four bar graphs, each of which has four bars, one for each of the years 1980, 1985, 1990, and 1995.

c. Which region had the greatest increase in numbers of people in the population from 1980 to 1995? Which region had the smallest increase in numbers of people in the population from 1980 to 1995?

d. Which region had the greatest increase in percentage of total population from 1980 to 1995? Which region had the greatest decline in percentage of total population from 1980 to 1995?

e. Write two or more comparison statements that describe the data for the four years.

f. Which statements below are true?

i. The South had the most people in each year.

ii. The population in the Northeast increased from 1980 to 1995.

iii. The percentage of population in the Northeast increased from 1980 to 1995.

iv. The distribution of population is more uneven in 1995 than in 1980.

Additional Practice (continued)

7. Make a line plot, matching the criteria below, to show the distribution of hand widths in a class:

There are 20 students in the class.

The range of hand widths is from 8 cm to 12.5 cm.

The mode hand width is 9.5 cm; there are 6 values at the mode.

The median hand width is 9 cm.

8. Make a line plot, matching the criteria below, to show the distribution of hand widths in a class:

There are 20 students in the class

The range of hand widths is from 8 cm to 12.5 cm.

The mode hand width is 9.5 cm; there are 6 values at the mode.

The median hand width is 10 cm.

Skill: Bar Graphs

For Exercises 1–3, use the table.

All-Time Favorite Sports Figures

Sports Figure	Votes
Babe Ruth	29
Babe Didrikson Zaharias	22
Jackie Robinson	18
Billie Jean Moffitt King	17
Muhammad Ali	14
Jim Thorpe	13

1. What would you label the horizontal axis for a bar graph of the data?

2. What interval would you use for the vertical axis of the bar graph?

3. Make a bar graph.

Skill: Line Plots

Data Distributions

Ms. Makita made a line plot to show the scores her students got on a test. At the right is Ms. Makita's line plot.

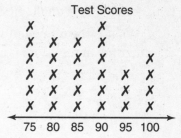

Test Scores

1. What does each data item or ✗ represent?

2. How many more students scored 75 than scored 95?

3. How many students scored over 85?

4. What scores did the same number of students get?

Use the line plot at the right for Exercises 5–7.

5. How many students spent time doing homework last night?

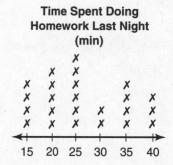

Time Spent Doing Homework Last Night (min)

6. How many students spent at least half an hour on homework?

7. What is the range of time spent on homework last night?

Additional Practice

1. Sandra's scores on the first 4 tests were 87, 92, 76, and 89.

  a. What is the minimum score Sandra needs to make on the fifth test so that her mean test score is at least 85? Explain.

  b. What is the minimum score Sandra needs to make on the fifth test so that her mean test score is at least 80? Explain.

  c. Can Sandra score well enough so that her mean score is 90 or above? Explain.

  d. If Sandra scores 100 on the fifth test, what is her median test score?

  e. If Sandra scores 0 on the fifth test, what is her median test score?

  f. What score or scores on the fifth test will give Sandra a median test score of 88? 87? 89?

Skill: Measures of Center

Each student in a class has taken five tests. The teacher allows the students to pick the mean, median, or mode of each set of scores to be their average. Which measure of center should each student pick in order to have the highest average?

1. 100, 87, 81, 23, 19

2. 90, 80, 74, 74, 72

3. 80, 80, 70, 67, 68

4. 75, 78, 77, 70, 70

5. 100, 47, 45, 32, 31

6. 86, 86, 77, 14, 12

7. 79, 78, 77, 76, 85

8. 86, 80, 79, 70, 70

Skill: Measures of Center (continued)

Use the tables for Exercises 9–14.

9. What is the mean height of the active volcanoes listed to the nearest foot?

10. What is the median height of the active volcanoes listed?

11. What is the mode of the heights of the active volcanoes listed?

12. What is the mean of the wages listed?

13. What is the median of the wages listed?

14. What is the mode of the wages listed?

Active Volcanoes

Name	Height Above Sea Level (ft)
Cameroon Mt.	13,354
Mount Erebus	12,450
Asama	8,300
Gerde	9,705
Sarychev	5,115
Ometepe	5,106
Fogo	9,300
Mt. Hood	11,245
Lascar	19,652

Hourly Wages of Production Workers in 1991 (includes benefits)

Country	Wage
Austria	$17.47
Brazil	$2.25
Finland	$20.57
France	$15.26
Hong Kong	$3.58
Japan	$14.41
Mexico	$2.17
Spain	$12.65
United States	$15.45

Additional Practice

1. Write three different statements that describe the variability in Leah's reaction times from the value bar graph.

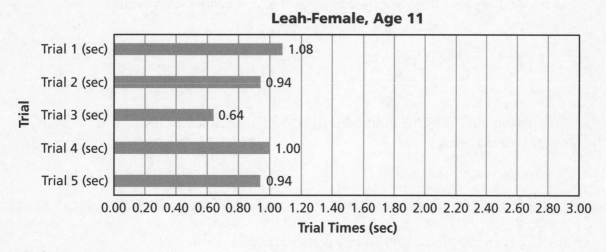

Leah-Female, Age 11

Trial	Trial Times (sec)
Trial 1 (sec)	1.08
Trial 2 (sec)	0.94
Trial 3 (sec)	0.64
Trial 4 (sec)	1.00
Trial 5 (sec)	0.94

2. Below is a value bar graph showing data about Ella's reaction times. Compare Ella's reaction times to Leah's reaction times.

a. Determine statistics for each student: means, medians, and ranges.

b. Is one student quicker than the other student? Explain your reasoning.

c. Is one student more consistent than the other student? Explain.

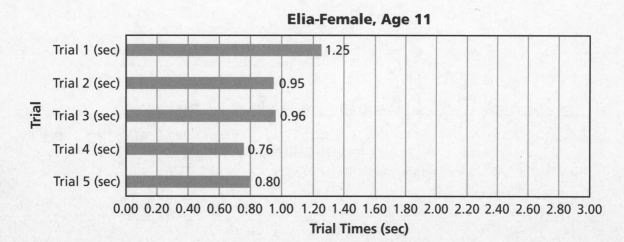

Elia-Female, Age 11

Trial	Trial Times (sec)
Trial 1 (sec)	1.25
Trial 2 (sec)	0.95
Trial 3 (sec)	0.96
Trial 4 (sec)	0.76
Trial 5 (sec)	0.80

Additional Practice *(continued)*

3. The sample of data below is about from 50 students – 25 female students and 25 male students. Two questions on a survey asked students to respond to a stimulus, once with their right hands and once with their left hands. Their time to respond is recorded in seconds. Below are two graphs, one for RIGHT hand and one for LEFT hand response data.

   a. Are students quicker with their right hands or their left hands? Justify your reasoning.

   b. Are students more consistent with their right hands or their left hands? Justify your reasoning.

   c. We have been using data that look at a person's dominant hand and non-dominant hand in the Investigation. Is it possible that, for some of the students, their right hand was their non-dominant hand? Explain.

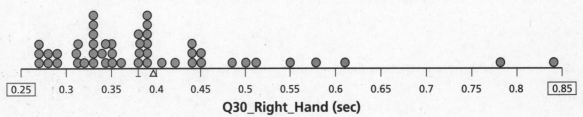

Q30_Right_Hand (sec)

The mean is 0.39702 sec and the median is 0.38 sec.

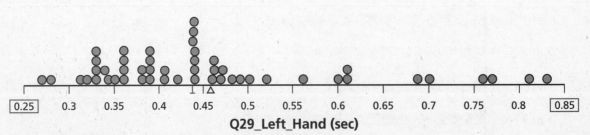

Q29_Left_Hand (sec)

The mean is 0.45726 sec and the median is 0.4375 sec.

SOURCE: www.censusonline.net

Additional Practice (continued)

4. Using the same data set about reaction times, compare the male reaction times with their right hands to the female reaction times with their right hands. Look at the graphs below.

Male

Female
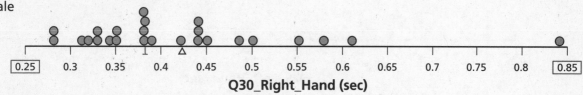

Q30_Right_Hand (sec)

Males: mean = 0.37124 sec and median = 0.344 sec
Females: mean = 0.4228 sec and median = 0.382 sec

a. For both females and males, their means and medians are different. What accounts for this happening?

b. Are females quicker than males using their right hands? Justify your reasoning.

c. Are females more consistent than males using their right hands? Justify your reasoning.

Additional Practice *(continued)*

5. Using the same data set about reaction times, compare the male reaction times with their left hands to the female reaction times with their left hands. Look at the graphs below.

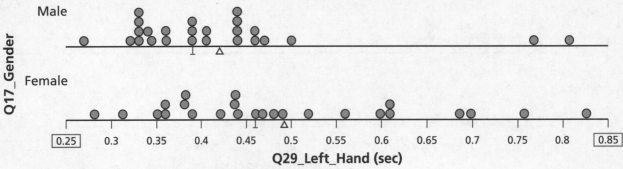

Males: mean = 0.42128 sec and median = 0.39 sec
Females: mean = 0.49324 sec and median = 0.461 sec

a. For both females and males, the means and medians are different. What might account for this happening?

b. Are females quicker than males using their left hands? Justify your reasoning.

c. Are females more consistent than males using their left hands? Justify your reasoning.

Additional Practice

1. Are wood coasters longer than steel coasters? Use the Roller Coaster Database and graphs below to help answer the question.

   Use these strategies and others that make sense to you:

   a. Compare statistics (ranges, medians, means) for each type of roller coaster.

   b. Partition the distributions at benchmark lengths and look at the percents of each type of roller coaster at and above or below this speed. For example, for *length* you could look at the percent of wood and percent steel roller coasters with lengths at and above or below 1,000 ft, 2,000 ft, 3,000 ft, 4,000 ft, and so on.

Steel Coasters

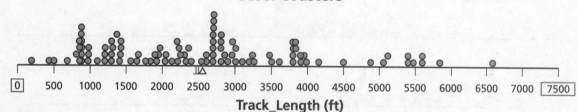

Mean = 2548, median = 2468.5, spread = 198–6595

Wood Coasters

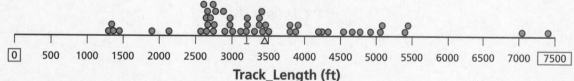

Mean = 3450.78, median = 3200, spread = 1800–7400

Additional Practice (continued)

2. Look at the graph showing track length and duration of rides for 150 roller coasters. Write three observations about the relationship between track length and duration of ride.

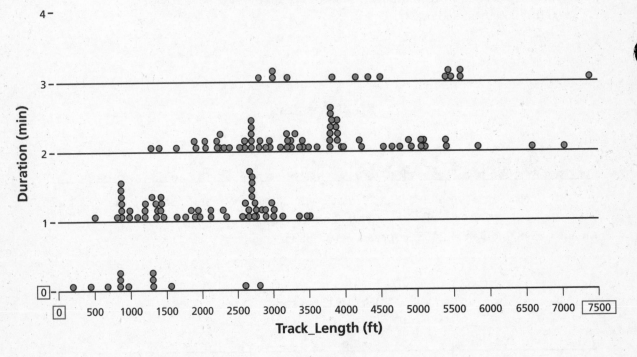

Roller Coasters: Track Length and Duration of Ride

Additional Practice *(continued)*

3. a. Use the table. When was the difference in numbers of boys and girls the greatest? The least?

b. When was the difference in the percent of boys and girls the greatest? The least?

Participation in Scouts (millions)

	Boys	Girls
1970	4.7	3.2
1975	3.9	2.7
1980	3.2	2.3
1985	3.8	2.2
1990	4.3	2.5
1995	4.3	2.5

4. Edwin was playing a game but wondered if the number cubes he was using were fair. He rolled the suspicious number cubes 36 times and found the sum of the two numbers on the top faces. Then he compared the results to rolls of fair number cubes that had been completed in his mathematics class.

Suspicious Rolls

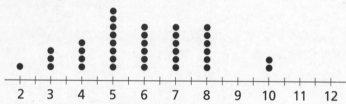

Fair Rolls

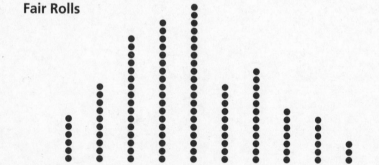

a. Write three statements comparing the distribution of sums for the two sets of number cubes.

b. Do you think the suspicious number cubes are fair? Explain your answer.